Opened Ground

Selected Poems

1966–1996

Seamus Heaney

Opened Ground

Selected Poems

1966–1996

Farrar, Straus and Giroux

New York

Farrar, Straus and Giroux
19 Union Square West, New York 10003

Printed in the United States of America
Designed by Cynthia Krupat
First published in 1998 by Faber and Faber Limited, as Poems: 1966–1996
First Farrar, Straus and Giroux edition, 1998
First Farrar, Straus and Giroux paperback edition, 1999

Library of Congress Cataloging-in-Publication Data
Heaney, Seamus.
    Opened ground : poems, 1966–1996 / Seamus Heaney. — 1st Farrar,
Straus and Giroux ed.
        p.   cm.
    Includes index.
    ISBN 0-374-52678-8 (pbk.)
    1. Ireland—Poetry.   I. Title
PR6058.E2065   1998
    821'.914—dc21   98-4331

for Marie

Author's Note

This book contains a greater number of poems than would usually appear in a *Selected Poems*, fewer than would make up a *Collected*: it belongs somewhere between the two categories.

I have taken the opportunity to include a very few poems not printed in previous volumes and made a short sequence of extracts from *The Cure at Troy* (1990), my version of Sophocles' *Philoctetes*. In similar fashion, 'Sweeney in Flight' is made up of sections from *Sweeney Astray* (1983), a translation of the medieval Irish work *Buile Suibhne*, which tells of the penitential life led by Sweeney after he was cursed and turned into a wild flying creature by St Ronan at the Battle of Moira.

Stations was published as a pamphlet by Ulsterman Publications in 1975. The first pieces were written in Berkeley in 1970.

'Station Island' is a sequence of dream encounters set on an island in County Donegal where, since medieval times, pilgrims have gone to perform the prescribed penitential exercises (or 'stations').

'Villanelle for an Anniversary' was written to commemorate the 350th anniversary of the founding of Harvard College in 1636. 'Alphabets' was the Phi Beta Kappa poem at Harvard in 1984.

I have included 'Crediting Poetry' as an Afterword. This seemed to make sense, since the ground covered in the lecture is ground originally opened by the poems which here precede it.

S.H.

Contents

from *Wintering Out*
(1972)

from *Stations*
(1975)

from *North*
(1975)

from *Sweeney Astray*
(1983)

from *Station Island*
(1984)

from *The Haw Lantern*
(1987)

from *The Spirit Level*
(1996)

Crediting Poetry
(1995)

FROM

Death of a Naturalist

[1 9 6 6]

Digging

Between my finger and my thumb
The squat pen rests; snug as a gun.

Under my window, a clean rasping sound
When the spade sinks into gravelly ground:
My father, digging. I look down

Till his straining rump among the flowerbeds
Bends low, comes up twenty years away
Stooping in rhythm through potato drills
Where he was digging.

The coarse boot nestled on the lug, the shaft
Against the inside knee was levered firmly.
He rooted out tall tops, buried the bright edge deep
To scatter new potatoes that we picked,
Loving their cool hardness in our hands.

By God, the old man could handle a spade.
Just like his old man.

My grandfather cut more turf in a day
Than any other man on Toner's bog.
Once I carried him milk in a bottle
Corked sloppily with paper. He straightened up
To drink it, then fell to right away
Nicking and slicing neatly, heaving sods
Over his shoulder, going down and down
For the good turf. Digging.

The cold smell of potato mould, the squelch and slap
Of soggy peat, the curt cuts of an edge
Through living roots awaken in my head.
But I've no spade to follow men like them.

Between my finger and my thumb
The squat pen rests.
I'll dig with it.

Death of a Naturalist

All year the flax-dam festered in the heart
Of the townland; green and heavy-headed
Flax had rotted there, weighted down by huge sods.
Daily it sweltered in the punishing sun.
Bubbles gargled delicately, bluebottles
Wove a strong gauze of sound around the smell.
There were dragonflies, spotted butterflies,
But best of all was the warm thick slobber
Of frogspawn that grew like clotted water
In the shade of the banks. Here, every spring
I would fill jampotfuls of the jellied
Specks to range on window-sills at home,
On shelves at school, and wait and watch until
The fattening dots burst into nimble-
Swimming tadpoles. Miss Walls would tell us how
The daddy frog was called a bullfrog
And how he croaked and how the mammy frog
Laid hundreds of little eggs and this was
Frogspawn. You could tell the weather by frogs too
For they were yellow in the sun and brown
In rain.

Then one hot day when fields were rank
With cowdung in the grass the angry frogs
Invaded the flax-dam; I ducked through hedges
To a coarse croaking that I had not heard
Before. The air was thick with a bass chorus.
Right down the dam gross-bellied frogs were cocked
On sods; their loose necks pulsed like sails. Some hopped:
The slap and plop were obscene threats. Some sat
Poised like mud grenades, their blunt heads farting.
I sickened, turned, and ran. The great slime kings
Were gathered there for vengeance and I knew
That if I dipped my hand the spawn would clutch it.

The Barn

Threshed corn lay piled like grit of ivory
Or solid as cement in two-lugged sacks.
The musky dark hoarded an armoury
Of farmyard implements, harness, plough-socks.

The floor was mouse-grey, smooth, chilly concrete.
There were no windows, just two narrow shafts
Of gilded motes, crossing, from air-holes slit
High in each gable. The one door meant no draughts

All summer when the zinc burned like an oven.
A scythe's edge, a clean spade, a pitchfork's prongs:
Slowly bright objects formed when you went in.
Then you felt cobwebs clogging up your lungs

And scuttled fast into the sunlit yard—
And into nights when bats were on the wing
Over the rafters of sleep, where bright eyes stared
From piles of grain in corners, fierce, unblinking.

The dark gulfed like a roof-space. I was chaff
To be pecked up when birds shot through the air-slits.
I lay face-down to shun the fear above.
The two-lugged sacks moved in like great blind rats.

Blackberry-Picking

for Philip Hobsbaum

Late August, given heavy rain and sun
For a full week, the blackberries would ripen.
At first, just one, a glossy purple clot
Among others, red, green, hard as a knot.
You ate that first one and its flesh was sweet
Like thickened wine: summer's blood was in it
Leaving stains upon the tongue and lust for
Picking. Then red ones inked up and that hunger
Sent us out with milk cans, pea tins, jam pots
Where briars scratched and wet grass bleached our boots.
Round hayfields, cornfields and potato drills
We trekked and picked until the cans were full,
Until the tinkling bottom had been covered
With green ones, and on top big dark blobs burned
Like a plate of eyes. Our hands were peppered
With thorn pricks, our palms sticky as Bluebeard's.

We hoarded the fresh berries in the byre
But when the bath was filled we found a fur,
A rat-grey fungus, glutting on our cache.
The juice was stinking too. Once off the bush
The fruit fermented, the sweet flesh would turn sour.
I always felt like crying. It wasn't fair
That all the lovely canfuls smelt of rot.
Each year I hoped they'd keep, knew they would not.

Churning Day

A thick crust, coarse-grained as limestone rough-cast,
hardened gradually on top of the four crocks
that stood, large pottery bombs, in the small pantry.
After the hot brewery of gland, cud and udder,
cool porous earthenware fermented the butter milk
for churning day, when the hooped churn was scoured
with plumping kettles and the busy scrubber
echoed daintily on the seasoned wood.
It stood then, purified, on the flagged kitchen floor.

Out came the four crocks, spilled their heavy lip
of cream, their white insides, into the sterile churn.
The staff, like a great whiskey muddler fashioned
in deal wood, was plunged in, the lid fitted.
My mother took first turn, set up rhythms
that slugged and thumped for hours. Arms ached.
Hands blistered. Cheeks and clothes were spattered
with flabby milk.

     Where finally gold flecks
began to dance. They poured hot water then,
sterilized a birchwood bowl
and little corrugated butter-spades.
Their short stroke quickened, suddenly
a yellow curd was weighting the churned-up white,
heavy and rich, coagulated sunlight
that they fished, dripping, in a wide tin strainer,
heaped up like gilded gravel in the bowl.

The house would stink long after churning day,
acrid as a sulphur mine. The empty crocks
were ranged along the wall again, the butter
in soft printed slabs was piled on pantry shelves.
And in the house we moved with gravid ease,

our brains turned crystals full of clean deal churns,
the plash and gurgle of the sour-breathed milk,
the pat and slap of small spades on wet lumps.

Follower

My father worked with a horse-plough,
His shoulders globed like a full sail strung
Between the shafts and the furrow.
The horses strained at his clicking tongue.

An expert. He would set the wing
And fit the bright steel-pointed sock.
The sod rolled over without breaking.
At the headrig, with a single pluck

Of reins, the sweating team turned round
And back into the land. His eye
Narrowed and angled at the ground,
Mapping the furrow exactly.

I stumbled in his hobnailed wake,
Fell sometimes on the polished sod;
Sometimes he rode me on his back
Dipping and rising to his plod.

I wanted to grow up and plough,
To close one eye, stiffen my arm.
All I ever did was follow
In his broad shadow round the farm.

I was a nuisance, tripping, falling,
Yapping always. But today
It is my father who keeps stumbling
Behind me, and will not go away.

Mid-Term Break

I sat all morning in the college sick bay
Counting bells knelling classes to a close.
At two o'clock our neighbours drove me home.

In the porch I met my father crying—
He had always taken funerals in his stride—
And Big Jim Evans saying it was a hard blow.

The baby cooed and laughed and rocked the pram
When I came in, and I was embarrassed
By old men standing up to shake my hand

And tell me they were 'sorry for my trouble'.
Whispers informed strangers I was the eldest,
Away at school, as my mother held my hand

In hers and coughed out angry tearless sighs.
At ten o'clock the ambulance arrived
With the corpse, stanched and bandaged by the nurses.

Next morning I went up into the room. Snowdrops
And candles soothed the bedside; I saw him
For the first time in six weeks. Paler now,

Wearing a poppy bruise on his left temple,
He lay in the four-foot box as in his cot.
No gaudy scars, the bumper knocked him clear.

A four-foot box, a foot for every year.

The Diviner

Cut from the green hedge a forked hazel stick
That he held tight by the arms of the V:
Circling the terrain, hunting the pluck
Of water, nervous, but professionally

Unfussed. The pluck came sharp as a sting.
The rod jerked with precise convulsions,
Spring water suddenly broadcasting
Through a green hazel its secret stations.

The bystanders would ask to have a try.
He handed them the rod without a word.
It lay dead in their grasp till, nonchalantly,
He gripped expectant wrists. The hazel stirred.

Poem

for Marie

Love, I shall perfect for you the child
Who diligently potters in my brain
Digging with heavy spade till sods were piled
Or puddling through muck in a deep drain.

Yearly I would sow my yard-long garden.
I'd strip a layer of sods to build the wall
That was to keep out sow and pecking hen.
Yearly, admitting these, the sods would fall.

Or in the sucking clabber I would splash
Delightedly and dam the flowing drain
But always my bastions of clay and mush
Would burst before the rising autumn rain.

Love, you shall perfect for me this child
Whose small imperfect limits would keep breaking:
Within new limits now, arrange the world
And square the circle: four walls and a ring.

Personal Helicon

for Michael Longley

As a child, they could not keep me from wells
And old pumps with buckets and windlasses.
I loved the dark drop, the trapped sky, the smells
Of waterweed, fungus and dank moss.

One, in a brickyard, with a rotted board top.
I savoured the rich crash when a bucket
Plummeted down at the end of a rope.
So deep you saw no reflection in it.

A shallow one under a dry stone ditch
Fructified like any aquarium.
When you dragged out long roots from the soft mulch
A white face hovered over the bottom.

Others had echoes, gave back your own call
With a clean new music in it. And one
Was scaresome, for there, out of ferns and tall
Foxgloves, a rat slapped across my reflection.

Now, to pry into roots, to finger slime,
To stare, big-eyed Narcissus, into some spring
Is beneath all adult dignity. I rhyme
To see myself, to set the darkness echoing.

Antaeus

When I lie on the ground
I rise flushed as a rose in the morning.
In fights I arrange a fall on the ring
  To rub myself with sand

That is operative
As an elixir. I cannot be weaned
Off the earth's long contour, her river-veins.
  Down here in my cave

Girdered with root and rock
I am cradled in the dark that wombed me
And nurtured in every artery
  Like a small hillock.

Let each new hero come
Seeking the golden apples and Atlas:
He must wrestle with me before he pass
  Into that realm of fame

Among sky-born and royal.
He may well throw me and renew my birth
But let him not plan, lifting me off the earth,
  My elevation, my fall.

FROM

Door into the Dark

[1 9 6 9]

The Outlaw

Kelly's kept an unlicensed bull, well away
From the road: you risked a fine but had to pay

The normal fee if cows were serviced there.
Once I dragged a nervous Friesian on a tether

Down a lane of alder, shaggy with catkin,
Down to the shed the bull was kept in.

I gave Old Kelly the clammy silver, though why
I could not guess. He grunted a curt 'Go by.

Get up on that gate.' And from my lofty station
I watched the businesslike conception.

The door, unbolted, whacked back against the wall.
The illegal sire fumbled from his stall

Unhurried as an old steam engine shunting.
He circled, snored and nosed. No hectic panting,

Just the unfussy ease of a good tradesman;
Then an awkward, unexpected jump, and

His knobbled forelegs straddling her flank,
He slammed life home, impassive as a tank,

Dropping off like a tipped-up load of sand.
'She'll do,' said Kelly and tapped his ashplant

Across her hindquarters. 'If not, bring her back.'
I walked ahead of her, the rope now slack

While Kelly whooped and prodded his outlaw
Who, in his own time, resumed the dark, the straw.

The Forge

All I know is a door into the dark.
Outside, old axles and iron hoops rusting;
Inside, the hammered anvil's short-pitched ring,
The unpredictable fantail of sparks
Or hiss when a new shoe toughens in water.
The anvil must be somewhere in the centre,
Horned as a unicorn, at one end square,
Set there immoveable: an altar
Where he expends himself in shape and music.
Sometimes, leather-aproned, hairs in his nose,
He leans out on the jamb, recalls a clatter
Of hoofs where traffic is flashing in rows;
Then grunts and goes in, with a slam and flick
To beat real iron out, to work the bellows.

Thatcher

Bespoke for weeks, he turned up some morning
Unexpectedly, his bicycle slung
With a light ladder and a bag of knives.
He eyed the old rigging, poked at the eaves,

Opened and handled sheaves of lashed wheat-straw.
Next, the bundled rods: hazel and willow
Were flicked for weight, twisted in case they'd snap.
It seemed he spent the morning warming up:

Then fixed the ladder, laid out well-honed blades
And snipped at straw and sharpened ends of rods
That, bent in two, made a white-pronged staple
For pinning down his world, handful by handful.

Couchant for days on sods above the rafters,
He shaved and flushed the butts, stitched all together
Into a sloped honeycomb, a stubble patch,
And left them gaping at his Midas touch.

The Peninsula

When you have nothing more to say, just drive
For a day all round the peninsula.
The sky is tall as over a runway,
The land without marks, so you will not arrive

But pass through, though always skirting landfall.
At dusk, horizons drink down sea and hill,
The ploughed field swallows the whitewashed gable
And you're in the dark again. Now recall

The glazed foreshore and silhouetted log,
That rock where breakers shredded into rags,
The leggy birds stilted on their own legs,
Islands riding themselves out into the fog,

And drive back home, still with nothing to say
Except that now you will uncode all landscapes
By this: things founded clean on their own shapes,
Water and ground in their extremity.

Requiem for the Croppies

The pockets of our greatcoats full of barley—
No kitchens on the run, no striking camp—
We moved quick and sudden in our own country.
The priest lay behind ditches with the tramp.
A people, hardly marching—on the hike—
We found new tactics happening each day:
We'd cut through reins and rider with the pike
And stampede cattle into infantry,
Then retreat through hedges where cavalry must be thrown.
Until, on Vinegar Hill, the fatal conclave.
Terraced thousands died, shaking scythes at cannon.
The hillside blushed, soaked in our broken wave.
They buried us without shroud or coffin
And in August the barley grew up out of the grave.

Undine

He slashed the briars, shovelled up grey silt
To give me right-of-way in my own drains
And I ran quick for him, cleaned out my rust.

He halted, saw me finally disrobed,
Running clear, with apparent unconcern.
Then he walked by me. I rippled and I churned

Where ditches intersected near the river
Until he dug a spade deep in my flank
And took me to him. I swallowed his trench

Gratefully, dispersing myself for love
Down in his roots, climbing his brassy grain—
But once he knew my welcome, I alone

Could give him subtle increase and reflection.
He explored me so completely, each limb
Lost its cold freedom. Human, warmed to him.

The Wife's Tale

When I had spread it all on linen cloth
Under the hedge, I called them over.
The hum and gulp of the thresher ran down
And the big belt slewed to a standstill, straw
Hanging undelivered in the jaws.
There was such quiet that I heard their boots
Crunching the stubble twenty yards away.

He lay down and said, 'Give these fellows theirs,
I'm in no hurry,' plucking grass in handfuls
And tossing it in the air. 'That looks well.'
(He nodded at my white cloth on the grass.)
'I declare a woman could lay out a field
Though boys like us have little call for cloths.'
He winked, then watched me as I poured a cup
And buttered the thick slices that he likes.
'It's threshing better than I thought, and mind
It's good clean seed. Away over there and look.'
Always this inspection has to be made
Even when I don't know what to look for.

But I ran my hand in the half-filled bags
Hooked to the slots. It was hard as shot,
Innumerable and cool. The bags gaped
Where the chutes ran back to the stilled drum
And forks were stuck at angles in the ground
As javelins might mark lost battlefields.
I moved between them back across the stubble.

They lay in the ring of their own crusts and dregs,
Smoking and saying nothing. 'There's good yield,
Isn't there?'—as proud as if he were the land itself—
'Enough for crushing and for sowing both.'
And that was it. I'd come and he had shown me,

So I belonged no further to the work.
I gathered cups and folded up the cloth
And went. But they still kept their ease,
Spread out, unbuttoned, grateful, under the trees.

Night Drive

The smells of ordinariness
Were new on the night drive through France:
Rain and hay and woods on the air
Made warm draughts in the open car.

Signposts whitened relentlessly.
Montreuil, Abbeville, Beauvais
Were promised, promised, came and went,
Each place granting its name's fulfilment.

A combine groaning its way late
Bled seeds across its work-light.
A forest fire smouldered out.
One by one small cafés shut.

I thought of you continuously
A thousand miles south where Italy
Laid its loin to France on the darkened sphere.
Your ordinariness was renewed there.

Relic of Memory

The lough waters
Can petrify wood:
Old oars and posts
Over the years
Harden their grain,
Incarcerate ghosts

Of sap and season.
The shallows lap
And give and take:
Constant ablutions,
Such a drowning love
Stun a stake

To stalagmite.
Dead lava,
The cooling star,
Coal and diamond
Or sudden birth
Of burnt meteor

Are too simple,
Without the lure
That relic stored—
A piece of stone
On the shelf at school,
Oatmeal coloured.

A Lough Neagh Sequence

for the fishermen

1. Up the Shore

I

The lough will claim a victim every year.
It has virtue that hardens wood to stone.
There is a town sunk beneath its water.
It is the scar left by the Isle of Man.

II

At Toomebridge where it sluices towards the sea
They've set new gates and tanks against the flow.
From time to time they break the eels' journey
And lift five hundred stone in one go.

III

But up the shore in Antrim and Tyrone
There is a sense of fair play in the game.
The fishermen confront them one by one
And sail miles out, and never learn to swim.

IV

'We'll be the quicker going down,' they say—
And when you argue there are no storms here,
That one hour floating's sure to land them safely—
'The lough will claim a victim every year.'

2. Beyond Sargasso

A gland agitating
mud two hundred miles in-
land, a scale of water
on water working up
estuaries, he drifted
into motion half-way
across the Atlantic,
sure as the satellite's
insinuating pull
in the ocean, as true
to his orbit.
    Against
ebb, current, rock, rapids,
a muscled icicle
that melts itself longer
and fatter, he buries
his arrival beyond
light and tidal water,
investing silt and sand
with a sleek root. By day
only the drainmaker's
spade or the mud paddler
can make him abort. Dark
delivers him hungering
down each undulation.

3. Bait

Lamps dawdle in the field at midnight.
Three men follow their nose in the grass,
The lamp's beam their prow and compass.

The bucket's handle better not clatter now:
Silence and curious light gather bait.
Nab him, but wait

For the first shrinking, tacky on the thumb.
Let him resettle backwards in his tunnel.
Then draw steady and he'll come.

Among the millions whorling their mud coronas
Under dewlapped leaf and bowed blades
A few are bound to be rustled in these night raids,

Innocent ventilators of the ground
Making the globe a perfect fit,
A few are bound to be cheated of it

When lamps dawdle in the field at midnight,
When fishers need a garland for the bay
And have him, where he needs to come, out of the clay.

4. Setting

I

A line goes out of sight and out of mind
Down to the soft bottom of silt and sand
Past the indifferent skill of the hunting hand.

A bouquet of small hooks coiled in the stern
Is being paid out, back to its true form,
Until the bouquet's hidden in the worm.

The boat rides forward where the line slants back.
The oars in their locks go round and round.
The eel describes his arcs without a sound.

II

The gulls fly and umbrella overhead,
Treading air as soon as the line runs out,
Responsive acolytes above the boat.

Not sensible of any *kyrie*,
The fishers, who don't know and never try,
Pursue the work in hand as destiny.

They clear the bucket of the last chopped worms,
Pitching them high, good riddance, earthy shower.
The gulls encompass them before the water.

5. Lifting

They're busy in a high boat
That stalks towards Antrim, the power cut.
The line's a filament of smut

Drawn hand over fist
Where every three yards a hook's missed
Or taken (and the smut thickens, wrist-

Thick, a flail
Lashed into the barrel
With one swing). Each eel

Comes aboard to this welcome:
The hook left in gill or gum,
It's slapped into the barrel numb

But knits itself, four-ply,
With the furling, slippy
Haul, a knot of back and pewter belly

That stays continuously one
For each catch they fling in
Is sucked home like lubrication.

And wakes are enwound as the catch
On the morning water: which
Boat was which?

And when did this begin?
This morning, last year, when the lough first spawned?
The crews will answer, 'Once the season's in.'

6. The Return

In ponds, drains, dead canals
she turns her head back,
older now, following
whim deliberately
till she's at sea in grass
and damned if she'll stop so
it's new trenches, sunk pipes,
swamps, running streams, the lough,
the river. Her stomach
shrunk, she exhilarates
in mid-water. Its throbbing
is speed through days and weeks.

Who knows now if she knows
her depth or direction?
She's passed Malin and
Tory, silent, wakeless,
a wisp, a wick that is
its own taper and light
through the weltering dark.
Where she's lost once she lays
ten thousand feet down in
her origins. The current
carries slicks of orphaned spawn.

7. *Vision*

Unless his hair was fine-combed
The lice, they said, would gang up
Into a mealy rope
And drag him, small, dirty, doomed,

Down to the water. He was
Cautious then in riverbank
Fields. Thick as a birch trunk,
That cable flexed in the grass

Every time the wind passed. Years
Later in the same fields
He stood at night when eels
Moved through the grass like hatched fears

Towards the water. To stand
In one place as the field flowed
Past, a jellied road,
To watch the eels crossing land

Re-wound his world's live girdle.
Phosphorescent, sinewed slime
Continued at his feet. Time
Confirmed the horrid cable.

The Given Note

On the most westerly Blasket
In a dry-stone hut
He got this air out of the night.

Strange noises were heard
By others who followed, bits of a tune
Coming in on loud weather

Though nothing like melody.
He blamed their fingers and ear
As unpractised, their fiddling easy

For he had gone alone into the island
And brought back the whole thing.
The house throbbed like his full violin.

So whether he calls it spirit music
Or not, I don't care. He took it
Out of wind off mid-Atlantic.

Still he maintains, from nowhere.
It comes off the bow gravely,
Rephrases itself into the air.

Whinlands

All year round the whin
Can show a blossom or two
But it's in full bloom now.
As if the small yolk stain

From all the birds' eggs in
All the nests of the spring
Were spiked and hung
Everywhere on bushes to ripen.

Hills oxidize gold.
Above the smoulder of green shoot
And dross of dead thorns underfoot
The blossoms scald.

Put a match under
Whins, they go up of a sudden.
They make no flame in the sun
But a fierce heat tremor

Yet incineration like that
Only takes the thorn.
The tough sticks don't burn,
Remain like bone, charred horn.

Gilt, jaggy, springy, frilled
This stunted, dry richness
Persists on hills, near stone ditches,
Over flintbed and battlefield.

The Plantation

Any point in that wood
Was a centre, birch trunks
Ghosting your bearings,
Improvising charmed rings

Wherever you stopped.
Though you walked a straight line
It might be a circle you travelled
With toadstools and stumps

Always repeating themselves.
Or did you re-pass them?
Here were bleyberries quilting the floor,
The black char of a fire,

And having found them once
You were sure to find them again.
Someone had always been there
Though always you were alone.

Lovers, birdwatchers,
Campers, gypsies and tramps
Left some trace of their trades
Or their excrement.

Hedging the road so
It invited all comers
To the hush and the mush
Of its whispering treadmill,

Its limits defined,
So they thought, from outside.
They must have been thankful
For the hum of the traffic

If they ventured in
Past the picnickers' belt
Or began to recall
Tales of fog on the mountains.

You had to come back
To learn how to lose yourself,
To be pilot and stray—witch,
Hansel and Gretel in one.

Bann Clay

Labourers pedalling at ease
Past the end of the lane
Were white with it. Dungarees
And boots wore its powdery stain.

All day in open pits
They loaded on to the bank
Slabs like the squared-off clots
Of a blue cream. Sunk

For centuries under the grass,
It baked white in the sun,
Relieved its hoarded waters
And began to ripen.

It underruns the valley,
The first slow residue
Of a river finding its way.
Above it, the webbed marsh is new,

Even the clutch of Mesolithic
Flints. Once, cleaning a drain
I shovelled up livery slicks
Till the water gradually ran

Clear on its old floor.
Under the humus and roots
This smooth weight. I labour
Towards it still. It holds and gluts.

Bogland

for T. P. Flanagan

We have no prairies
To slice a big sun at evening—
Everywhere the eye concedes to
Encroaching horizon,

Is wooed into the cyclops' eye
Of a tarn. Our unfenced country
Is bog that keeps crusting
Between the sights of the sun.

They've taken the skeleton
Of the Great Irish Elk
Out of the peat, set it up,
An astounding crate full of air.

Butter sunk under
More than a hundred years
Was recovered salty and white.
The ground itself is kind, black butter

Melting and opening underfoot,
Missing its last definition
By millions of years.
They'll never dig coal here,

Only the waterlogged trunks
Of great firs, soft as pulp.
Our pioneers keep striking
Inwards and downwards,

Every layer they strip
Seems camped on before.
The bogholes might be Atlantic seepage.
The wet centre is bottomless.

FROM

Wintering Out

[1 9 7 2]

Fodder

Or, as we said,
fother, I open
my arms for it
again. But first

to draw from the tight
vise of a stack
the weathered eaves
of the stack itself

falling at your feet,
last summer's tumbled
swathes of grass
and meadowsweet

multiple as loaves
and fishes, a bundle
tossed over half-doors
or into mucky gaps.

These long nights
I would pull hay
for comfort, anything
to bed the stall.

Bog Oak

A carter's trophy
split for rafters,
a cobwebbed, black,
long-seasoned rib

under the first thatch.
I might tarry
with the moustached
dead, the creel-fillers,

or eavesdrop on
their hopeless wisdom
as a blow-down of smoke
struggles over the half-door

and mizzling rain
blurs the far end
of the cart track.
The softening ruts

lead back to no
'oak groves', no
cutters of mistletoe
in the green clearings.

Perhaps I just make out
Edmund Spenser,
dreaming sunlight,
encroached upon by

geniuses who creep
'out of every corner
of the woodes and glennes'
towards watercress and carrion.

Anahorish

My 'place of clear water',
the first hill in the world
where springs washed into
the shiny grass

and darkened cobbles
in the bed of the lane.
Anahorish, soft gradient
of consonant, vowel-meadow,

after-image of lamps
swung through the yards
on winter evenings.
With pails and barrows

those mound-dwellers
go waist-deep in mist
to break the light ice
at wells and dunghills.

Servant Boy

He is wintering out
the back-end of a bad year,
swinging a hurricane-lamp
through some outhouse,

a jobber among shadows.
Old work-whore, slave-
blood, who stepped fair-hills
under each bidder's eye

and kept your patience
and your counsel, how
you draw me into
your trail. Your trail

broken from haggard to stable,
a straggle of fodder
stiffened on snow,
comes first-footing

the back doors of the little
barons: resentful
and impenitent,
carrying the warm eggs.

Land

I stepped it, perch by perch.
Unbraiding rushes and grass
I opened my right-of-way
through old bottoms and sowed-out ground
and gathered stones off the ploughing
to raise a small cairn.
Cleaned out the drains, faced the hedges,
often got up at dawn
to walk the outlying fields.

I composed habits for those acres
so that my last look would be
neither gluttonous nor starved.
I was ready to go anywhere.

II

This is in place of what I would leave,
plaited and branchy,
on a long slope of stubble:

a woman of old wet leaves,
rush-bands and thatcher's scollops,
stooked loosely, her breasts an open-work

of new straw and harvest bows.
Gazing out past
the shifting hares.

III

I sense the pads
unfurling under grass and clover:

if I lie with my ear
in this loop of silence

long enough, thigh-bone
and shoulder against the phantom ground,

I expect to pick up
a small drumming

and must not be surprised
in bursting air

to find myself snared, swinging
an ear-ring of sharp wire.

Gifts of Rain

I

Cloudburst and steady downpour now
for days.
        Still mammal,
straw-footed on the mud,
he begins to sense weather
by his skin.

A nimble snout of flood
licks over stepping stones
and goes uprooting.
            He fords
his life by sounding.
               Soundings.

II

A man wading lost fields
breaks the pane of flood:

a flower of mud-
water blooms up to his reflection

like a cut swaying
its red spoors through a basin.

His hands grub
where the spade has uncastled

sunken drills, an atlantis
he depends on. So

he is hooped to where he planted
and sky and ground

are running naturally among his arms
that grope the cropping land.

III

When rains were gathering
there would be an all-night
roaring off the ford.
Their world-schooled ear

could monitor the usual
confabulations, the race
slabbering past the gable,
the Moyola harping on

its gravel beds:
all spouts by daylight
brimmed with their own airs
and overflowed each barrel

in long tresses.
I cock my ear
at an absence—
in the shared calling of blood

arrives my need
for antediluvian lore.
Soft voices of the dead
are whispering by the shore

that I would question
(and for my children's sake)
about crops rotted, river mud
glazing the baked clay floor.

IV

The tawny guttural water
spells itself: Moyola
is its own score and consort,

bedding the locale
in the utterance,
reed music, an old chanter

breathing its mists
through vowels and history.
A swollen river,

a mating call of sound
rises to pleasure me, Dives,
hoarder of common ground.

Toome

My mouth holds round
the soft blastings,
Toome, Toome,
as under the dislodged

slab of the tongue
I push into a souterrain
prospecting what new
in a hundred centuries'

loam, flints, musket-balls,
fragmented ware,
torcs and fish-bones,
till I am sleeved in

alluvial mud that shelves
suddenly under
bogwater and tributaries,
and elvers tail my hair.

Broagh

Riverbank, the long rigs
ending in broad docken
and a canopied pad
down to the ford.

The garden mould
bruised easily, the shower
gathering in your heelmark
was the black *O*

in *Broagh*,
its low tattoo
among the windy boortrees
and rhubarb-blades

ended almost
suddenly, like that last
gh the strangers found
difficult to manage.

Oracle

Hide in the hollow trunk
of the willow tree,
its listening familiar,
until, as usual, they
cuckoo your name
across the fields.
You can hear them
draw the poles of stiles
as they approach
calling you out:
small mouth and ear
in a woody cleft,
lobe and larynx
of the mossy places.

The Backward Look

A stagger in air
as if a language
failed, a sleight
of wing.

A snipe's bleat is fleeing
its nesting-ground
into dialect,
into variants,

transliterations whirr
on the nature reserves—
little goat of the air,
of the evening,

little goat of the frost.
It is his tail-feathers
drumming elegies
in the slipstream

of wild goose
and yellow bittern
as he corkscrews away
into the vaults

that we live off, his flight
through the sniper's eyrie,
over twilit earthworks
and wallsteads,

disappearing among
gleanings and leavings
in the combs
of a fieldworker's archive.

A New Song

I met a girl from Derrygarve
And the name, a lost potent musk,
Recalled the river's long swerve,
A kingfisher's blue bolt at dusk

And stepping stones like black molars
Sunk in the ford, the shifty glaze
Of the whirlpool, the Moyola
Pleasuring beneath alder trees.

And Derrygarve, I thought, was just:
Vanished music, twilit water—
A smooth libation of the past
Poured by this chance vestal daughter.

But now our river tongues must rise
From licking deep in native haunts
To flood, with vowelling embrace,
Demesnes staked out in consonants.

And Castledawson we'll enlist
And Upperlands, each planted bawn—
Like bleaching-greens resumed by grass—
A vocable, as rath and bullaun.

The Other Side

I

Thigh-deep in sedge and marigolds,
a neighbour laid his shadow
on the stream, vouching

'It's as poor as Lazarus, that ground,'
and brushed away
among the shaken leafage.

I lay where his lea sloped
to meet our fallow,
nested on moss and rushes,

my ear swallowing
his fabulous, biblical dismissal,
that tongue of chosen people.

When he would stand like that
on the other side, white-haired,
swinging his blackthorn

at the marsh weeds,
he prophesied above our scraggy acres,
then turned away

towards his promised furrows
on the hill, a wake of pollen
drifting to our bank, next season's tares.

II

For days we would rehearse
each patriarchal dictum:
Lazarus, the Pharaoh, Solomon

and David and Goliath rolled
magnificently, like loads of hay
too big for our small lanes,

or faltered on a rut—
'Your side of the house, I believe,
hardly rule by the Book at all.'

His brain was a whitewashed kitchen
hung with texts, swept tidy
as the body o' the kirk.

III

Then sometimes when the rosary was dragging
mournfully on in the kitchen
we would hear his step round the gable

though not until after the litany
would the knock come to the door
and the casual whistle strike up

on the doorstep. 'A right-looking night,'
he might say, 'I was dandering by
and says I, I might as well call.'

But now I stand behind him
in the dark yard, in the moan of prayers.
He puts a hand in a pocket

or taps a little tune with the blackthorn
shyly, as if he were party to
lovemaking or a stranger's weeping.

Should I slip away, I wonder,
or go up and touch his shoulder
and talk about the weather

or the price of grass-seed?

Tinder

(from *A Northern Hoard*)

We picked flints,
Pale and dirt-veined,

So small finger and thumb
Ached around them;

Cold beads of history and home
We fingered, a cave-mouth flame

Of leaf and stick
Trembling at the mind's wick.

We clicked stone on stone
That sparked a weak flame-pollen

And failed, our knuckle joints
Striking as often as the flints.

What did we know then
Of tinder, charred linen and iron,

Huddled at dusk in a ring,
Our fists shut, our hope shrunken?

What could strike a blaze
From our dead igneous days?

Now we squat on cold cinder,
Red-eyed, after the flames' soft thunder

And our thoughts settle like ash.
We face the tundra's whistling brush

With new history, flint and iron,
Cast-offs, scraps, nail, canine.

The Tollund Man

Some day I will go to Aarhus
To see his peat-brown head,
The mild pods of his eyelids,
His pointed skin cap.

In the flat country nearby
Where they dug him out,
His last gruel of winter seeds
Caked in his stomach,

Naked except for
The cap, noose and girdle,
I will stand a long time.
Bridegroom to the goddess,

She tightened her torc on him
And opened her fen,
Those dark juices working
Him to a saint's kept body,

Trove of the turf-cutters'
Honeycombed workings.
Now his stained face
Reposes at Aarhus.

I could risk blasphemy,
Consecrate the cauldron bog
Our holy ground and pray
Him to make germinate

The scattered, ambushed
Flesh of labourers,
Stockinged corpses
Laid out in the farmyards,

Tell-tale skin and teeth
Flecking the sleepers
Of four young brothers, trailed
For miles along the lines.

III

Something of his sad freedom
As he rode the tumbril
Should come to me, driving,
Saying the names

Tollund, Grauballe, Nebelgard,
Watching the pointing hands
Of country people,
Not knowing their tongue.

Out there in Jutland
In the old man-killing parishes
I will feel lost,
Unhappy and at home.

Nerthus

For beauty, say an ash-fork staked in peat,
Its long grains gathering to the gouged split;

A seasoned, unsleeved taker of the weather
Where kesh and loaning finger out to heather.

Wedding Day

I am afraid.
Sound has stopped in the day
And the images reel over
And over. Why all those tears,

The wild grief on his face
Outside the taxi? The sap
Of mourning rises
In our waving guests.

You sing behind the tall cake
Like a deserted bride
Who persists, demented,
And goes through the ritual.

When I went to the Gents
There was a skewered heart
And a legend of love. Let me
Sleep on your breast to the airport.

Mother of the Groom

What she remembers
Is his glistening back
In the bath, his small boots
In the ring of boots at her feet.

Hands in her voided lap,
She hears a daughter welcomed.
It's as if he kicked when lifted
And slipped her soapy hold.

Once soap would ease off
The wedding ring
That's bedded forever now
In her clapping hand.

Summer Home

I

Was it wind off the dumps
or something in heat

dogging us, the summer gone sour,
a fouled nest incubating somewhere?

Whose fault, I wondered, inquisitor
of the possessed air.

To realize suddenly,
whip off the mat

that was larval, moving—
and scald, scald, scald.

II

Bushing the door, my arms full
of wild cherry and rhododendron,
I hear her small lost weeping
through the hall, that bells and hoarsens
on my name, my name.

O love, here is the blame.

The loosened flowers between us
gather in, compose
for a May altar of sorts.
These frank and falling blooms
soon taint to a sweet chrism.

Attend. Anoint the wound.

III

Oh we tented our wound all right
under the homely sheet

and lay as if the cold flat of a blade
had winded us.

More and more I postulate
thick healings, like now

as you bend in the shower
water lives down the tilting stoups of your breasts.

IV

With a final
unmusical drive
long grains begin
to open and split

ahead and once more
we sap
the white, trodden
path to the heart.

V

My children weep out the hot foreign night.
We walk the floor, my foul mouth takes it out
On you and we lie stiff till dawn
Attends the pillow, and the maize, and vine

That holds its filling burden to the light.
Yesterday rocks sang when we tapped
Stalactites in the cave's old, dripping dark—
Our love calls tiny as a tuning fork.

Serenades

The Irish nightingale
Is a sedge-warbler,
A little bird with a big voice
Kicking up a racket all night.

Not what you'd expect
From the musical nation.
I haven't even heard one—
Nor an owl, for that matter.

My serenades have been
The broken voice of a crow
In a draught or a dream,
The wheeze of bats

Or the ack-ack
Of the tramp corncrake
Lost in a no-man's-land
Between combines and chemicals.

So fill the bottles, love,
Leave them inside their cots,
And if they do wake us, well,
So would the sedge-warbler.

Shore Woman

Man to the hills, woman to the shore.
   —GAELIC PROVERB

I have crossed the dunes with their whistling bent
Where dry loose sand was riddling round the air
And I'm walking the firm margin. White pocks
Of cockle, blanched roofs of clam and oyster
Hoard the moonlight, woven and unwoven
Off the bay. At the far rocks
A pale sud comes and goes.

Under boards the mackerel slapped to death
Yet still we took them in at every cast,
Stiff flails of cold convulsed with their first breath.
My line plumbed certainly the undertow,
Loaded against me once I went to draw
And flashed and fattened up towards the light.
He was all business in the stern. I called
'This is so easy that it's hardly right,'
But he unhooked and coped with frantic fish
Without speaking. Then suddenly it lulled,
We'd crossed where they were running, the line rose
Like a let-down and I was conscious
How far we'd drifted out beyond the head.
'Count them up at your end,' was all he said
Before I saw the porpoises' thick backs
Cartwheeling like the flywheels of the tide,
Soapy and shining. To have seen a hill
Splitting the water could not have numbed me more
Than the close irruption of that school,
Tight viscous muscle, hooped from tail to snout,
Each one revealed complete as it bowled out
And under.
          They will attack a boat.
I knew it and asked him to put in

But he would not, declared it was a yarn
My people had been fooled by far too long
And he would prove it now and settle it.
Maybe he shrank when those sloped oily backs
Propelled towards us: I lay and screamed
Under splashed brine in an open rocking boat,
Feeling each dunt and slither through the timber,
Sick at their huge pleasures in the water.

I sometimes walk this strand for thanksgiving
Or maybe it's to get away from him
Skittering his spit across the stove. Here
Is the taste of safety, the shelving sand
Harbours no worse than razor-shell or crab—
Though my father recalls carcasses of whales
Collapsed and gasping, right up to the dunes.
But tonight such moving sinewed dreams lie out
In darker fathoms, far beyond the head.
Astray upon a debris of scrubbed shells
Between parched dunes and salivating wave,
I have rights on this fallow avenue,
A membrane between moonlight and my shadow.

Limbo

Fishermen at Ballyshannon
Netted an infant last night
Along with the salmon.
An illegitimate spawning,

A small one thrown back
To the waters. But I'm sure
As she stood in the shallows
Ducking him tenderly

Till the frozen knobs of her wrists
Were dead as the gravel,
He was a minnow with hooks
Tearing her open.

She waded in under
The sign of her cross.
He was hauled in with the fish.
Now limbo will be

A cold glitter of souls
Through some far briny zone.
Even Christ's palms, unhealed,
Smart and cannot fish there.

Bye-Child

He was discovered in the henhouse where she had confined him.
He was incapable of saying anything.

When the lamp glowed,
A yolk of light
In their back window,
The child in the outhouse
Put his eye to a chink—

Little henhouse boy,
Sharp-faced as new moons
Remembered, your photo still
Glimpsed like a rodent
On the floor of my mind,

Little moon man,
Kennelled and faithful
At the foot of the yard,
Your frail shape, luminous,
Weightless, is stirring the dust,

The cobwebs, old droppings
Under the roosts
And dry smells from scraps
She put through your trapdoor
Morning and evening.

After those footsteps, silence;
Vigils, solitudes, fasts,
Unchristened tears,
A puzzled love of the light.
But now you speak at last

With a remote mime
Of something beyond patience,
Your gaping wordless proof
Of lunar distances
Travelled beyond love.

Good-night

A latch lifting, an edged den of light
Opens across the yard. Out of the low door
They stoop into the honeyed corridor,
Then walk straight through the wall of the dark.

A puddle, cobble-stones, jambs and doorstep
Are set steady in a block of brightness.
Till she strides in again beyond her shadows
And cancels everything behind her.

Fireside

Always there would be stories of lights
hovering among bushes or at the foot
of a meadow; maybe a goat with cold horns
pluming into the moon; a tingle of chains

on the midnight road. And then maybe
word would come round of that watery
art, the lamping of fishes, and I'd be
mooning my flashlamp on the licked black pelt

of the stream, my left arm splayed to take
a heavy pour and run of the current
occluding the net. Was that the beam
buckling over an eddy or a gleam

of the fabulous? Steady the light
and come to your senses, they're saying good-night.

Westering

in California

I sit under Rand McNally's
'Official Map of the Moon'—
The colour of frogskin,
Its enlarged pores held

Open and one called
'Pitiscus' at eye level—
Recalling the last night
In Donegal, my shadow

Neat upon the whitewash
From her bony shine,
The cobbles of the yard
Lit pale as eggs.

Summer had been a free fall
Ending there,
The empty amphitheatre
Of the west. Good Friday

We had started out
Past shopblinds drawn on the afternoon,
Cars stilled outside still churches,
Bikes tilting to a wall;

We drove by,
A dwindling interruption,
As clappers smacked
On a bare altar

And congregations bent
To the studded crucifix.
What nails dropped out that hour?
Roads unreeled, unreeled

Falling light as casts
Laid down
On shining waters.
Under the moon's stigmata

Six thousand miles away,
I imagine untroubled dust,
A loosening gravity,
Christ weighing by his hands.

FROM

Stations

[1 9 7 5]

Nesting-Ground

The sandmartins' nests were loopholes of darkness in the riverbank. He could imagine his arm going in to the armpit, sleeved and straitened, but because he had once felt the cold prick of a dead robin's claw and the surprising density of its tiny beak he only gazed.

He heard cheeping far in but because the men had once shown him a rat's nest in the butt of a stack where chaff and powdered cornstalks adhered to the moist pink necks and backs he only listened.

As he stood sentry, gazing, waiting, he thought of putting his ear to one of the abandoned holes and listening for the silence under the ground.

July

The drumming started in the cool of the evening, as if the dome of air were lightly hailed on. But no. The drumming murmured from beneath that drum.

The drumming didn't murmur, rather hammered. Sound-smiths found a rhythm gradually. On the far bench of the hills tuns and ingots were being beaten thin.

The hills were a bellied sound-box resonating, a low dyke against diurnal roar, a tidal wave that stayed, that still might open.

Through red seas of July the Orange drummers led a chosen people through their dream. Dilations and engorgings, contrapuntal; slashers in shirt-sleeves, collared in the sunset, policemen flanking them like anthracite.

The air grew dark, cloud-barred, a butcher's apron. The night hushed like a white-mothed reach of water, miles downstream from the battle, a skein of blood still lazing in the channel.

England's Difficulty

I moved like a double agent among the big concepts. The word 'enemy' had the toothed efficiency of a mowing machine. It was a mechanical and distant noise beyond that opaque security, that autonomous ignorance. 'When the Germans bombed Belfast it was the bitterest Orange parts were hit the worst.'

I was on somebody's shoulder, conveyed through the starlit yard to see the sky glowing over Anahorish. Grown-ups lowered their voices and resettled in the kitchen as if tired out after an excursion.

Behind the blackout, Germany called to lamplit kitchens through fretted baize, dry battery, wet battery, capillary wires, domed valves that squeaked and burbled as the dial-hand absolved Stuttgart and Leipzig.

'He's an artist, this Haw Haw. He can fairly leave it into them.'

I lodged with 'the enemies of Ulster', the scullions outside the walls. An adept at banter, I crossed the lines with carefully enunciated passwords, manned every speech with checkpoints and reported back to nobody.

Visitant

It kept treading air, as if it were a ghost with claims on us, precipitating in the heat tremor. Then, released from its distorting mirror, up the fields there comes this awkwardly smiling foreigner, awkwardly received, who gentled the long Sunday afternoon just by sitting with us.

Where are you now, real visitant, who vivified 'parole' and 'POW'? Where are the rings garnetted with bits of toothbrush, the ships in bottles, the Tyrol landscapes globed in electric bulbs?

'They've hands for anything, these Germans.'

He walked back into the refining lick of the grass, behind the particular judgements of captor and harbourer. As he walks yet, feeling our eyes on his back, treading the air of the image he achieved, released to his fatigues.

Trial Runs

WELCOME HOME YE LADS OF THE EIGHTH ARMY. There had to be some defiance in it because it was painted along the demesne wall, a banner headline over the old news of REMEMBER 1690 and NO SURRENDER, a great wingspan of lettering I hurried under with the messages.

In a khaki shirt and brass-buckled belt, a demobbed neighbour leaned against our jamb. My father jingled silver deep in both pockets and laughed when the big clicking rosary beads were produced.

'Did they make a Papish of you over there?'

'Oh damn the fear! I stole them for you, Paddy, off the Pope's dresser when his back was turned.'

'You could harness a donkey with them.'

Their laughter sailed above my head, a hoarse clamour, two big nervous birds dipping and lifting, making trial runs across a territory.

The Wanderer

In a semicircle we toed the line chalked round the master's desk
and on a day when the sun was incubating milktops and warm-
ing the side of the jam jar where the bean had split its stitches,
he called me forward and crossed my palm with silver. 'At the
end of the holidays this man's going away to Derry, so this is
for him, for winning the scholarship . . . We all wish him good
luck. Now, back to your places.'

I have wandered far from that ring-giver and would not
renegue on this migrant solitude. I have seen halls in flames,
hearts in cinders, the benches filled and emptied, the circles of
companions called and broken. That day I was a rich young
man, who could tell you now of flittings, night-vigils, let-downs,
women's cried-out eyes.

Cloistered

Light was calloused in the leaded panes of the college chapel and shafted into the terrazzo rink of the sanctuary. The duty priest tested his diction against pillar and plaster, we tested our elbows on the hard bevel of the benches or split the gold-barred thickness of our missals.

I could make a book of hours of those six years, a Flemish calendar of rite and pastime set on a walled hill. Look: there is a hillside cemetery behind us and across the river the plough going in a field and, in between, the gated town. Here, an obedient clerk kissing a bishop's ring, here a frieze of seasonal games, and here the assiduous illuminator himself, bowed to his desk in a corner.

In the study hall my hand was cold as a scribe's in winter. The supervisor rustled past, sibilant, vapouring into his breviary, his welted brogues unexpectedly secular under the soutane. Now I bisected the line AB, now found my foothold in a main verb in Livy. From my dormer after lights out I revised the constellations and in the morning broke the ice in an enamelled water-jug with exhilarated self-regard.

The Stations of the West

On my first night in the Gaeltacht the old woman spoke to me
in English: 'You will be all right.' I sat on a twilit bedside
listening through the wall to fluent Irish, homesick for a speech
I was to extirpate.

I had come west to inhale the absolute weather. The vi-
sionaries breathed on my face a smell of soup-kitchens, they
mixed the dust of croppies' graves with the fasting spittle of our
creed and anointed my lips. *Ephete*, they urged. I blushed but
only managed a few words.

Neither did any gift of tongues descend in my days in that
upper room when all around me seemed to prophesy. But still
I would recall the stations of the west, white sand, hard rock,
light ascending like its definition over Rannafast and Errigal,
Annaghry and Kincasslagh: names portable as altar stones, un-
leavened elements.

Incertus

I went disguised in it, pronouncing it with a soft church-Latin
c, tagging it under my efforts like a damp fuse. Uncertain. A
shy soul fretting and all that. Expert obeisance.
    Oh yes, I crept before I walked. The old pseudonym lies
there like a mouldering tegument.

F R O M

North

[1 9 7 5]

Mossbawn: Two Poems in Dedication

for Mary Heaney

1. Sunlight

There was a sunlit absence.
The helmeted pump in the yard
heated its iron,
water honeyed

in the slung bucket
and the sun stood
like a griddle cooling
against the wall

of each long afternoon.
So, her hands scuffled
over the bakeboard,
the reddening stove

sent its plaque of heat
against her where she stood
in a floury apron
by the window.

Now she dusts the board
with a goose's wing,
now sits, broad-lapped,
with whitened nails

and measling shins:
here is a space
again, the scone rising
to the tick of two clocks.

And here is love
like a tinsmith's scoop
sunk past its gleam
in the meal-bin.

2. The Seed Cutters

They seem hundreds of years away. Brueghel,
You'll know them if I can get them true.
They kneel under the hedge in a half-circle
Behind a windbreak wind is breaking through.
They are the seed cutters. The tuck and frill
Of leaf-sprout is on the seed potatoes
Buried under that straw. With time to kill,
They are taking their time. Each sharp knife goes
Lazily halving each root that falls apart
In the palm of the hand: a milky gleam,
And, at the centre, a dark watermark.
Oh, calendar customs! Under the broom
Yellowing over them, compose the frieze
With all of us there, our anonymities.

Funeral Rites

I shouldered a kind of manhood
stepping in to lift the coffins
of dead relations.
They had been laid out

in tainted rooms,
their eyelids glistening,
their dough-white hands
shackled in rosary beads.

Their puffed knuckles
had unwrinkled, the nails
were darkened, the wrists
obediently sloped.

The dulse-brown shroud,
the quilted satin cribs:
I knelt courteously
admiring it all

as wax melted down
and veined the candles,
the flames hovering
to the women hovering

behind me.
And always, in a corner,
the coffin lid,
its nail-heads dressed

with little gleaming crosses.
Dear soapstone masks,

kissing their igloo brows
had to suffice

before the nails were sunk
and the black glacier
of each funeral
pushed away.

II

Now as news comes in
of each neighbourly murder
we pine for ceremony,
customary rhythms:

the temperate footsteps
of a cortège, winding past
each blinded home.
I would restore

the great chambers of Boyne,
prepare a sepulchre
under the cupmarked stones.
Out of side-streets and by-roads

purring family cars
nose into line,
the whole country tunes
to the muffled drumming

of ten thousand engines.
Somnambulant women,
left behind, move
through emptied kitchens

imagining our slow triumph
towards the mounds.
Quiet as a serpent
in its grassy boulevard,

the procession drags its tail
out of the Gap of the North
as its head already enters
the megalithic doorway.

III

When they have put the stone
back in its mouth
we will drive north again
past Strang and Carling fjords,

the cud of memory
allayed for once, arbitration
of the feud placated,
imagining those under the hill

disposed like Gunnar
who lay beautiful
inside his burial mound,
though dead by violence

and unavenged.
Men said that he was chanting
verses about honour
and that four lights burned

in corners of the chamber:
which opened then, as he turned
with a joyful face
to look at the moon.

North

I returned to a long strand,
the hammered curve of a bay,
and found only the secular
powers of the Atlantic thundering.

I faced the unmagical
invitations of Iceland,
the pathetic colonies
of Greenland, and suddenly

those fabulous raiders,
those lying in Orkney and Dublin
measured against
their long swords rusting,

those in the solid
belly of stone ships,
those hacked and glinting
in the gravel of thawed streams

were ocean-deafened voices
warning me, lifted again
in violence and epiphany.
The longship's swimming tongue

was buoyant with hindsight—
it said Thor's hammer swung
to geography and trade,
thick-witted couplings and revenges,

the hatreds and behind-backs
of the althing, lies and women,
exhaustions nominated peace,
memory incubating the spilled blood.

It said, 'Lie down
in the word-hoard, burrow
the coil and gleam
of your furrowed brain.

Compose in darkness.
Expect aurora borealis
in the long foray
but no cascade of light.

Keep your eye clear
as the bleb of the icicle,
trust the feel of what nubbed treasure
your hands have known.'

Viking Dublin: Trial Pieces

I

It could be a jaw-bone
or a rib or a portion cut
from something sturdier:
anyhow, a small outline

was incised, a cage
or trellis to conjure in.
Like a child's tongue
following the toils

of his calligraphy,
like an eel swallowed
in a basket of eels,
the line amazes itself

eluding the hand
that fed it,
a bill in flight,
a swimming nostril.

II

These are trial pieces,
the craft's mystery
improvised on bone:
foliage, bestiaries,

interlacings elaborate
as the netted routes
of ancestry and trade.
That have to be

magnified on display
so that the nostril
is a migrant prow
sniffing the Liffey,

swanning it up to the ford,
dissembling itself
in antler combs, bone pins,
coins, weights, scale-pans.

III

Like a long sword
sheathed in its moisting
burial clays,
the keel stuck fast

in the slip of the bank,
its clinker-built hull
spined and plosive
as *Dublin.*

And now we reach in
for shards of the vertebrae,
the ribs of hurdle,
the mother-wet caches—

and for this trial piece
incised by a child,
a longship, a buoyant
migrant line.

IV

That enters my longhand,
turns cursive, unscarfing
a zoomorphic wake,
a worm of thought

I follow into the mud.
I am Hamlet the Dane,
skull-handler, parablist,
smeller of rot

in the state, infused
with its poisons,
pinioned by ghosts
and affections,

murders and pieties,
coming to consciousness
by jumping in graves,
dithering, blathering.

V

Come fly with me,
come sniff the wind
with the expertise
of the Vikings—

neighbourly, scoretaking
killers, haggers
and hagglers, gombeen-men,
hoarders of grudges and gain.

With a butcher's aplomb
they spread out your lungs
and made you warm wings
for your shoulders.

Old fathers, be with us.
Old cunning assessors
of feuds and of sites
for ambush or town.

VI

'Did you ever hear tell,'
said Jimmy Farrell,
'of the skulls they have
in the city of Dublin?

White skulls and black skulls
and yellow skulls, and some
with full teeth, and some
haven't only but one,'

and compounded history
in the pan of 'an old Dane,
maybe, was drowned
in the Flood.'

My words lick around
cobbled quays, go hunting
lightly as pampooties
over the skull-capped ground.

Bone Dreams

I

White bone found
on the grazing:
the rough, porous
language of touch

and its yellowing, ribbed
impression in the grass—
a small ship-burial.
As dead as stone,

flint-find, nugget
of chalk,
I touch it again,
I wind it in

the sling of mind
to pitch it at England
and follow its drop
to strange fields.

II

Bone-house:
a skeleton
in the tongue's
old dungeons.

I push back
through dictions,
Elizabethan canopies,
Norman devices,

the erotic mayflowers
of Provence
and the ivied Latins
of churchmen

to the scop's
twang, the iron
flash of consonants
cleaving the line.

III

In the coffered
riches of grammar
and declensions
I found *bān-hūs*,

its fire, benches,
wattle and rafters,
where the soul
fluttered a while

in the roofspace.
There was a small crock
for the brain,
and a cauldron

of generation
swung at the centre:
love-den, blood-holt,
dream-bower.

IV

Come back past
philology and kennings,
re-enter memory
where the bone's lair

is a love-nest
in the grass.
I hold my lady's head
like a crystal

and ossify myself
by gazing: I am screes
on her escarpments,
a chalk giant

carved upon her downs.
Soon my hands, on the sunken
fosse of her spine,
move towards the passes.

        V

And we end up
cradling each other
between the lips
of an earthwork.

As I estimate
for pleasure
her knuckles' paving,
the turning stiles

of the elbows,
the vallum of her brow
and the long wicket
of collar-bone,

I have begun to pace
the Hadrian's Wall
of her shoulder, dreaming
of Maiden Castle.

VI

One morning in Devon
I found a dead mole
with the dew still beading it.
I had thought the mole

a big-boned coulter
but there it was,
small and cold
as the thick of a chisel.

I was told, 'Blow,
blow back the fur on his head.
Those little points
were the eyes.

And feel the shoulders.'
I touched small distant Pennines,
a pelt of grass and grain
running south.

Bog Queen

I lay waiting
between turf-face and demesne wall,
between heathery levels
and glass-toothed stone.

My body was braille
for the creeping influences:
dawn suns groped over my head
and cooled at my feet,

through my fabrics and skins
the seeps of winter
digested me,
the illiterate roots

pondered and died
in the cavings
of stomach and socket.
I lay waiting

on the gravel bottom,
my brain darkening,
a jar of spawn
fermenting underground

dreams of Baltic amber.
Bruised berries under my nails,
the vital hoard reducing
in the crock of the pelvis.

My diadem grew carious,
gemstones dropped
in the peat floe
like the bearings of history.

My sash was a black glacier
wrinkling, dyed weaves
and Phoenician stitchwork
retted on my breasts'

soft moraines.
I knew winter cold
like the nuzzle of fjords
at my thighs—

the soaked fledge, the heavy
swaddle of hides.
My skull hibernated
in the wet nest of my hair.

Which they robbed.
I was barbered
and stripped
by a turf-cutter's spade

who veiled me again
and packed coomb softly
between the stone jambs
at my head and my feet.

Till a peer's wife bribed him.
The plait of my hair,
a slimy birth-cord
of bog, had been cut

and I rose from the dark,
hacked bone, skull-ware,
frayed stitches, tufts,
small gleams on the bank.

The Grauballe Man

As if he had been poured
in tar, he lies
on a pillow of turf
and seems to weep

the black river of himself.
The grain of his wrists
is like bog oak,
the ball of his heel

like a basalt egg.
His instep has shrunk
cold as a swan's foot
or a wet swamp root.

His hips are the ridge
and purse of a mussel,
his spine an eel arrested
under a glisten of mud.

The head lifts,
the chin is a visor
raised above the vent
of his slashed throat

that has tanned and toughened.
The cured wound
opens inwards to a dark
elderberry place.

Who will say 'corpse'
to his vivid cast?
Who will say 'body'
to his opaque repose?

And his rusted hair,
a mat unlikely
as a foetus's.
I first saw his twisted face

in a photograph,
a head and shoulder
out of the peat,
bruised like a forceps baby,

but now he lies
perfected in my memory,
down to the red horn
of his nails,

hung in the scales
with beauty and atrocity:
with the Dying Gaul
too strictly compassed

on his shield,
with the actual weight
of each hooded victim,
slashed and dumped.

III

Punishment

I can feel the tug
of the halter at the nape
of her neck, the wind
on her naked front.

It blows her nipples
to amber beads,
it shakes the frail rigging
of her ribs.

I can see her drowned
body in the bog,
the weighing stone,
the floating rods and boughs.

Under which at first
she was a barked sapling
that is dug up
oak-bone, brain-firkin:

her shaved head
like a stubble of black corn,
her blindfold a soiled bandage,
her noose a ring

to store
the memories of love.
Little adulteress,
before they punished you

you were flaxen-haired,
undernourished, and your
tar-black face was beautiful.
My poor scapegoat,

I almost love you
but would have cast, I know,
the stones of silence.
I am the artful voyeur

of your brain's exposed
and darkened combs,
your muscles' webbing
and all your numbered bones:

I who have stood dumb
when your betraying sisters,
cauled in tar,
wept by the railings,

who would connive
in civilized outrage
yet understand the exact
and tribal, intimate revenge.

Strange Fruit

Here is the girl's head like an exhumed gourd.
Oval-faced, prune-skinned, prune-stones for teeth.
They unswaddled the wet fern of her hair
And made an exhibition of its coil,
Let the air at her leathery beauty.
Pash of tallow, perishable treasure:
Her broken nose is dark as a turf clod,
Her eyeholes blank as pools in the old workings.
Diodorus Siculus confessed
His gradual ease among the likes of this:
Murdered, forgotten, nameless, terrible
Beheaded girl, outstaring axe
And beatification, outstaring
What had begun to feel like reverence.

Kinship

I

Kinned by hieroglyphic
peat on a spreadfield
to the strangled victim,
the love-nest in the bracken,

I step through origins
like a dog turning
its memories of wilderness
on the kitchen mat:

the bog floor shakes,
water cheeps and lisps
as I walk down
rushes and heather.

I love this turf-face,
its black incisions,
the cooped secrets
of process and ritual;

I love the spring
off the ground,
each bank a gallows drop,
each open pool

the unstopped mouth
of an urn, a moon-drinker,
not to be sounded
by the naked eye.

II

Quagmire, swampland, morass:
the slime kingdoms,

domains of the cold-blooded,
of mud pads and dirtied eggs.

But *bog*
meaning soft,
the fall of windless rain,
pupil of amber.

Ruminant ground,
digestion of mollusc
and seed-pod,
deep pollen-bin.

Earth-pantry, bone-vault,
sun-bank, embalmer
of votive goods
and sabred fugitives.

Insatiable bride.
Sword-swallower,
casket, midden,
floe of history.

Ground that will strip
its dark side.
Nesting ground.
Outback of my mind.

III

I found a turf-spade
hidden under bracken,
laid flat, and overgrown
with a green fog.

As I raised it
the soft lips of the growth
muttered and split,
a tawny rut

opening at my feet
like a shed skin,
the shaft wettish
as I sank it upright

and beginning to
steam in the sun.
And now they have twinned
that obelisk:

among the stones,
under a bearded cairn
a love-nest is disturbed,
catkin and bog-cotton tremble

as they raise up
the cloven oak-limb.
I stand at the edge of centuries
facing a goddess.

IV

This centre holds
and spreads,
sump and seedbed,
a bag of waters

and a melting grave.
The mothers of autumn
sour and sink,
ferments of husk and leaf

deepen their ochres.
Mosses come to a head,
heather unseeds,
brackens deposit

their bronze.
This is the vowel of earth

dreaming its root
in flowers and snow,

mutation of weathers
and seasons,
a windfall composing
the floor it rots into.

I grew out of all this
like a weeping willow
inclined to
the appetites of gravity.

V

The hand-carved felloes
of the turf-cart wheels
buried in a litter
of turf mould,

the cupid's bow
of the tail-board,
the socketed lips
of the cribs:

I deified the man
who rode there,
god of the waggon,
the hearth-feeder.

I was his privileged
attendant, a bearer
of bread and drink,
the squire of his circuits.

When summer died
and wives forsook the fields
we were abroad,
saluted, given right-of-way.

Watch our progress
down the haw-lit hedges,
my manly pride
when he speaks to me.

VI

And you, Tacitus,
observe how I make my grove
on an old crannog
piled by the fearful dead:

a desolate peace.
Our mother ground
is sour with the blood
of her faithful,

they lie gargling
in her sacred heart
as the legions stare
from the ramparts.

Come back to this
'island of the ocean'
where nothing will suffice.
Read the inhumed faces

of casualty and victim;
report us fairly,
how we slaughter
for the common good

and shave the heads
of the notorious,
how the goddess swallows
our love and terror.

Act of Union

I

Tonight, a first movement, a pulse,
As if the rain in bogland gathered head
To slip and flood: a bog-burst,
A gash breaking open the ferny bed.
Your back is a firm line of eastern coast
And arms and legs are thrown
Beyond your gradual hills. I caress
The heaving province where our past has grown.
I am the tall kingdom over your shoulder
That you would neither cajole nor ignore.
Conquest is a lie. I grow older
Conceding your half-independent shore
Within whose borders now my legacy
Culminates inexorably.

II

And I am still imperially
Male, leaving you with the pain,
The rending process in the colony,
The battering ram, the boom burst from within.
The act sprouted an obstinate fifth column
Whose stance is growing unilateral.
His heart beneath your heart is a wardrum
Mustering force. His parasitical
And ignorant little fists already
Beat at your borders and I know they're cocked
At me across the water. No treaty
I foresee will salve completely your tracked
And stretchmarked body, the big pain
That leaves you raw, like opened ground, again.

Hercules and Antaeus

Sky-born and royal,
snake-choker, dung-heaver,
his mind big with golden apples,
his future hung with trophies,

Hercules has the measure
of resistance and black powers
feeding off the territory.
Antaeus, the mould-hugger,

is weaned at last:
a fall was a renewal
but now he is raised up—
the challenger's intelligence

is a spur of light,
a blue prong graiping him
out of his element
into a dream of loss

and origins—the cradling dark,
the river-veins, the secret gullies
of his strength,
the hatching grounds

of cave and souterrain,
he has bequeathed it all
to elegists. Balor will die
and Byrthnoth and Sitting Bull.

Hercules lifts his arms
in a remorseless V,
his triumph unassailed
by the powers he has shaken,

and lifts and banks Antaeus
high as a profiled ridge,
a sleeping giant,
pap for the dispossessed.

from *Whatever You Say Say Nothing*

I'm writing this just after an encounter
With an English journalist in search of 'views
On the Irish thing'. I'm back in winter
Quarters where bad news is no longer news,

Where media-men and stringers sniff and point,
Where zoom lenses, recorders and coiled leads
Litter the hotels. The times are out of joint
But I incline as much to rosary beads

As to the jottings and analyses
Of politicians and newspapermen
Who've scribbled down the long campaign from gas
And protest to gelignite and Sten,

Who proved upon their pulses 'escalate',
'Backlash' and 'crack down', 'the provisional wing',
'Polarization' and 'long-standing hate'.
Yet I live here, I live here too, I sing,

Expertly civil-tongued with civil neighbours
On the high wires of first wireless reports,
Sucking the fake taste, the stony flavours
Of those sanctioned, old, elaborate retorts:

'Oh, it's disgraceful, surely, I agree.'
'Where's it going to end?' 'It's getting worse.'
'They're murderers.' 'Internment, understandably . . .'
The 'voice of sanity' is getting hoarse.

'Religion's never mentioned here,' of course.
'You know them by their eyes,' and hold your tongue.
'One side's as bad as the other,' never worse.
Christ, it's near time that some small leak was sprung

In the great dykes the Dutchman made
To dam the dangerous tide that followed Seamus.
Yet for all this art and sedentary trade
I am incapable. The famous

Northern reticence, the tight gag of place
And times: yes, yes. Of the 'wee six' I sing
Where to be saved you only must save face
And whatever you say, you say nothing.

Smoke-signals are loud-mouthed compared with us:
Manoeuvrings to find out name and school,
Subtle discrimination by addresses
With hardly an exception to the rule

That Norman, Ken and Sidney signalled Prod
And Seamus (call me Sean) was sure-fire Pape.
O land of password, handgrip, wink and nod,
Of open minds as open as a trap,

Where tongues lie coiled, as under flames lie wicks,
Where half of us, as in a wooden horse,
Were cabin'd and confined like wily Greeks,
Besieged within the siege, whispering morse.

IV

This morning from a dewy motorway
I saw the new camp for the internees:
A bomb had left a crater of fresh clay
In the roadside, and over in the trees

Machine-gun posts defined a real stockade.
There was that white mist you get on a low ground
And it was déjà-vu, some film made
Of Stalag 17, a bad dream with no sound.

Is there a life before death? That's chalked up
In Ballymurphy. Competence with pain,
Coherent miseries, a bite and sup:
We hug our little destiny again.

Singing School

Fair seedtime had my soul, and I grew up
Fostered alike by beauty and by fear;
Much favoured in my birthplace, and no less
In that beloved Vale to which, erelong,
I was transplanted . . .

—WILLIAM WORDSWORTH, *The Prelude*

He [the stable-boy] had a book of Orange rhymes, and the days when we read
them together in the hay-loft gave me the pleasure of rhyme for the first time.
Later on I can remember being told, when there was a rumour of a Fenian
rising, that rifles were being handed out to the Orangemen; and presently, when
I began to dream of my future life, I thought I would like to die fighting the
Fenians.

—W. B. YEATS, *Autobiographies*

1. The Ministry of Fear

for Seamus Deane

Well, as Kavanagh said, we have lived
In important places. The lonely scarp
Of St Columb's College, where I billeted
For six years, overlooked your Bogside.
I gazed into new worlds: the inflamed throat
Of Brandywell, its floodlit dogtrack,
The throttle of the hare. In the first week
I was so homesick I couldn't even eat
The biscuits left to sweeten my exile.
I threw them over the fence one night
In September 1951
When the lights of houses in the Lecky Road
Were amber in the fog. It was an act
Of stealth.
                    Then Belfast, and then Berkeley.
Here's two on's are sophisticated,

Dabbling in verses till they have become
A life: from bulky envelopes arriving
In vacation time to slim volumes
Despatched 'with the author's compliments'.
Those poems in longhand, ripped from the wire spine
Of your exercise book, bewildered me—
Vowels and ideas bandied free
As the seed-pods blowing off our sycamores.
I tried to write about the sycamores
And innovated a South Derry rhyme
With *hushed* and *lulled* full chimes for *pushed* and *pulled*.
Those hobnailed boots from beyond the mountain
Were walking, by God, all over the fine
Lawns of elocution.
                         Have our accents
Changed? 'Catholics, in general, don't speak
As well as students from the Protestant schools.'
Remember that stuff? Inferiority
Complexes, stuff that dreams were made on.
'What's your name, Heaney?'
                                    'Heaney, Father.'
                                                      'Fair
Enough.'
            On my first day, the leather strap
Went epileptic in the Big Study,
Its echoes plashing over our bowed heads,
But I still wrote home that a boarder's life
Was not so bad, shying as usual.

On long vacations, then, I came to life
In the kissing seat of an Austin 16
Parked at a gable, the engine running,
My fingers tight as ivy on her shoulders,
A light left burning for her in the kitchen.
And heading back for home, the summer's
Freedom dwindling night by night, the air
All moonlight and a scent of hay, policemen
Swung their crimson flashlamps, crowding round
The car like black cattle, snuffing and pointing

The muzzle of a Sten gun in my eye:
'What's your name, driver?'
                              'Seamus . . .'
                                        Seamus?
They once read my letters at a roadblock
And shone their torches on your hieroglyphics,
'Svelte dictions' in a very florid hand.

Ulster was British, but with no rights on
The English lyric: all around us, though
We hadn't named it, the ministry of fear.

2. A Constable Calls

His bicycle stood at the window-sill,
The rubber cowl of a mud-splasher
Skirting the front mudguard,
Its fat black handlegrips

Heating in sunlight, the 'spud'
Of the dynamo gleaming and cocked back,
The pedal treads hanging relieved
Of the boot of the law.

His cap was upside down
On the floor, next his chair.
The line of its pressure ran like a bevel
In his slightly sweating hair.

He had unstrapped
The heavy ledger, and my father
Was making tillage returns
In acres, roods, and perches.

Arithmetic and fear.
I sat staring at the polished holster
With its buttoned flap, the braid cord
Looped into the revolver butt.

'Any other root crops?
Mangolds? Marrowstems? Anything like that?'
'No.' But was there not a line
Of turnips where the seed ran out

In the potato field? I assumed
Small guilts and sat
Imagining the black hole in the barracks.
He stood up, shifted the baton-case

Farther round on his belt,
Closed the domesday book,
Fitted his cap back with two hands,
And looked at me as he said goodbye.

A shadow bobbed in the window.
He was snapping the carrier spring
Over the ledger. His boot pushed off
And the bicycle ticked, ticked, ticked.

3. Orange Drums, Tyrone, 1966

The lambeg balloons at his belly, weighs
Him back on his haunches, lodging thunder
Grossly there between his chin and his knees.
He is raised up by what he buckles under.

Each arm extended by a seasoned rod,
He parades behind it. And though the drummers
Are granted passage through the nodding crowd,
It is the drums preside, like giant tumours.

To every cocked ear, expert in its greed,
His battered signature subscribes 'No Pope'.
The goatskin's sometimes plastered with his blood.
The air is pounding like a stethoscope.

4. Summer 1969

While the Constabulary covered the mob
Firing into the Falls, I was suffering
Only the bullying sun of Madrid.
Each afternoon, in the casserole heat
Of the flat, as I sweated my way through
The life of Joyce, stinks from the fishmarket
Rose like the reek off a flax-dam.
At night on the balcony, gules of wine,
A sense of children in their dark corners,
Old women in black shawls near open windows,
The air a canyon rivering in Spanish.
We talked our way home over starlit plains
Where patent leather of the Guardia Civil
Gleamed like fish-bellies in flax-poisoned waters.

'Go back,' one said, 'try to touch the people.'
Another conjured Lorca from his hill.
We sat through death-counts and bullfight reports
On the television, celebrities
Arrived from where the real thing still happened.

I retreated to the cool of the Prado.
Goya's 'Shootings of the Third of May'
Covered a wall—the thrown-up arms
And spasm of the rebel, the helmeted
And knapsacked military, the efficient
Rake of the fusillade. In the next room,
His nightmares, grafted to the palace wall—
Dark cyclones, hosting, breaking; Saturn
Jewelled in the blood of his own children,
Gigantic Chaos turning his brute hips
Over the world. Also, that holmgang
Where two berserks club each other to death
For honour's sake, greaved in a bog, and sinking.

He painted with his fists and elbows, flourished
The stained cape of his heart as history charged.

5. *Fosterage*

for Michael McLaverty

'Description is revelation!' Royal
Avenue, Belfast, 1962,
A Saturday afternoon, glad to meet
Me, newly cubbed in language, he gripped
My elbow. 'Listen. Go your own way.
Do your own work. Remember
Katherine Mansfield—*I will tell
How the laundry basket squeaked* . . . that note of exile.'
But to hell with overstating it:
'Don't have the veins bulging in your Biro.'
And then, 'Poor Hopkins!' I have the *Journals*
He gave me, underlined, his buckled self
Obeisant to their pain. He discerned
The lineaments of patience everywhere
And fostered me and sent me out, with words
Imposing on my tongue like obols.

6. Exposure

It is December in Wicklow:
Alders dripping, birches
Inheriting the last light,
The ash tree cold to look at.

A comet that was lost
Should be visible at sunset,
Those million tons of light
Like a glimmer of haws and rose-hips,

And I sometimes see a falling star.
If I could come on meteorite!
Instead I walk through damp leaves,
Husks, the spent flukes of autumn,

Imagining a hero
On some muddy compound,
His gift like a slingstone
Whirled for the desperate.

How did I end up like this?
I often think of my friends'
Beautiful prismatic counselling
And the anvil brains of some who hate me

As I sit weighing and weighing
My responsible *tristia*.
For what? For the ear? For the people?
For what is said behind-backs?

Rain comes down through the alders,
Its low conducive voices
Mutter about let-downs and erosions
And yet each drop recalls

The diamond absolutes.
I am neither internee nor informer;
An inner émigré, grown long-haired
And thoughtful; a wood-kerne

Escaped from the massacre,
Taking protective colouring
From bole and bark, feeling
Every wind that blows;

Who, blowing up these sparks
For their meagre heat, have missed
The once-in-a-lifetime portent,
The comet's pulsing rose.

FROM

Field Work

[1 9 7 9]

Oysters

Our shells clacked on the plates.
My tongue was a filling estuary,
My palate hung with starlight:
As I tasted the salty Pleiades
Orion dipped his foot into the water.

Alive and violated
They lay on their beds of ice:
Bivalves: the split bulb
And philandering sigh of ocean.
Millions of them ripped and shucked and scattered.

We had driven to that coast
Through flowers and limestone
And there we were, toasting friendship,
Laying down a perfect memory
In the cool of thatch and crockery.

Over the Alps, packed deep in hay and snow,
The Romans hauled their oysters south to Rome:
I saw damp panniers disgorge
The frond-lipped, brine-stung
Glut of privilege

And was angry that my trust could not repose
In the clear light, like poetry or freedom
Leaning in from sea. I ate the day
Deliberately, that its tang
Might quicken me all into verb, pure verb.

Triptych

After a Killing

There they were, as if our memory hatched them,
As if the unquiet founders walked again:
Two young men with rifles on the hill,
Profane and bracing as their instruments.

Who's sorry for our trouble?
Who dreamt that we might dwell among ourselves
In rain and scoured light and wind-dried stones?
Basalt, blood, water, headstones, leeches.

In that neuter original loneliness
From Brandon to Dunseverick
I think of small-eyed survivor flowers,
The pined-for, unmolested orchid.

I see a stone house by a pier.
Elbow room. Broad window light.
The heart lifts. You walk twenty yards
To the boats and buy mackerel.

And today a girl walks in home to us
Carrying a basket full of new potatoes,
Three tight green cabbages, and carrots
With the tops and mould still fresh on them.

Sibyl

My tongue moved, a swung relaxing hinge.
I said to her, 'What will become of us?'
And as forgotten water in a well might shake
At an explosion under morning

Or a crack run up a gable,
She began to speak.
'I think our very form is bound to change.
Dogs in a siege. Saurian relapses. Pismires.

Unless forgiveness finds its nerve and voice,
Unless the helmeted and bleeding tree
Can green and open buds like infants' fists
And the fouled magma incubate

Bright nymphs . . . My people think money
And talk weather. Oil-rigs lull their future
On single acquisitive stems. Silence
Has shoaled into the trawlers' echo-sounders.

The ground we kept our ear to for so long
Is flayed or calloused, and its entrails
Tented by an impious augury.
Our island is full of comfortless noises.'

At the Water's Edge

On Devenish I heard a snipe
And the keeper's recital of elegies
Under the tower. Carved monastic heads
Were crumbling like bread on water.

On Boa the god-eyed, sex-mouthed stone
Socketed between graves, two-faced, trepanned,
Answered my silence with silence.
A stoup for rain water. Anathema.

From a cold hearthstone on Horse Island
I watched the sky beyond the open chimney
And listened to the thick rotations
Of an army helicopter patrolling.

A hammer and a cracked jug full of cobwebs
Lay on the window-sill. Everything in me
Wanted to bow down, to offer up,
To go barefoot, foetal and penitential,

And pray at the water's edge.
How we crept before we walked! I remembered
The helicopter shadowing our march at Newry,
The scared, irrevocable steps.

The Toome Road

One morning early I met armoured cars
In convoy, warbling along on powerful tyres,
All camouflaged with broken alder branches,
And headphoned soldiers standing up in turrets.
How long were they approaching down my roads
As if they owned them? The whole country was sleeping.
I had rights-of-way, fields, cattle in my keeping,
Tractors hitched to buckrakes in open sheds,
Silos, chill gates, wet slates, the greens and reds
Of outhouse roofs. Whom should I run to tell
Among all of those with their back doors on the latch
For the bringer of bad news, that small-hours visitant
Who, by being expected, might be kept distant?
Sowers of seed, erectors of headstones . . .
O charioteers, above your dormant guns,
It stands here still, stands vibrant as you pass,
The invisible, untoppled omphalos.

A Drink of Water

She came every morning to draw water
Like an old bat staggering up the field:
The pump's whooping cough, the bucket's clatter
And slow diminuendo as it filled,
Announced her. I recall
Her grey apron, the pocked white enamel
Of the brimming bucket, and the treble
Creak of her voice like the pump's handle.
Nights when a full moon lifted past her gable
It fell back through her window and would lie
Into the water set out on the table.
Where I have dipped to drink again, to be
Faithful to the admonishment on her cup,
Remember the Giver, fading off the lip.

The Strand at Lough Beg

in memory of Colum McCartney

All round this little island, on the strand
Far down below there, where the breakers strive,
Grow the tall rushes from the oozy sand.
—DANTE, *Purgatorio, I, 100–3*

Leaving the white glow of filling stations
And a few lonely streetlamps among fields
You climbed the hills towards Newtownhamilton
Past the Fews Forest, out beneath the stars—
Along that road, a high, bare pilgrim's track
Where Sweeney fled before the bloodied heads,
Goat-beards and dogs' eyes in a demon pack
Blazing out of the ground, snapping and squealing.
What blazed ahead of you? A faked roadblock?
The red lamp swung, the sudden brakes and stalling
Engine, voices, heads hooded and the cold-nosed gun?
Or in your driving mirror, tailing headlights
That pulled out suddenly and flagged you down
Where you weren't known and far from what you knew:
The lowland clays and waters of Lough Beg,
Church Island's spire, its soft treeline of yew.

There you once heard guns fired behind the house
Long before rising time, when duck shooters
Haunted the marigolds and bulrushes,
But still were scared to find spent cartridges,
Acrid, brassy, genital, ejected,
On your way across the strand to fetch the cows.
For you and yours and yours and mine fought shy,
Spoke an old language of conspirators
And could not crack the whip or seize the day:
Big-voiced scullions, herders, feelers round
Haycocks and hindquarters, talkers in byres,
Slow arbitrators of the burial ground.

Across that strand of yours the cattle graze
Up to their bellies in an early mist
And now they turn their unbewildered gaze
To where we work our way through squeaking sedge
Drowning in dew. Like a dull blade with its edge
Honed bright, Lough Beg half-shines under the haze.
I turn because the sweeping of your feet
Has stopped behind me, to find you on your knees
With blood and roadside muck in your hair and eyes,
Then kneel in front of you in brimming grass
And gather up cold handfuls of the dew
To wash you, cousin. I dab you clean with moss
Fine as the drizzle out of a low cloud.
I lift you under the arms and lay you flat.
With rushes that shoot green again, I plait
Green scapulars to wear over your shroud.

Casualty

I

He would drink by himself
And raise a weathered thumb
Towards the high shelf,
Calling another rum
And blackcurrant, without
Having to raise his voice,
Or order a quick stout
By a lifting of the eyes
And a discreet dumb-show
Of pulling off the top;
At closing time would go
In waders and peaked cap
Into the showery dark,
A dole-kept breadwinner
But a natural for work.
I loved his whole manner,
Sure-footed but too sly,
His deadpan sidling tact,
His fisherman's quick eye
And turned, observant back.

Incomprehensible
To him, my other life.
Sometimes, on his high stool,
Too busy with his knife
At a tobacco plug
And not meeting my eye,
In the pause after a slug
He mentioned poetry.
We would be on our own
And, always politic
And shy of condescension,

I would manage by some trick
To switch the talk to eels
Or lore of the horse and cart
Or the Provisionals.

But my tentative art
His turned back watches too:
He was blown to bits
Out drinking in a curfew
Others obeyed, three nights
After they shot dead
The thirteen men in Derry.
PARAS THIRTEEN, the walls said,
BOGSIDE NIL. That Wednesday
Everybody held
Their breath and trembled.

II

It was a day of cold
Raw silence, windblown
Surplice and soutane:
Rained-on, flower-laden
Coffin after coffin
Seemed to float from the door
Of the packed cathedral
Like blossoms on slow water.
The common funeral
Unrolled its swaddling band,
Lapping, tightening
Till we were braced and bound
Like brothers in a ring.

But he would not be held
At home by his own crowd
Whatever threats were phoned,
Whatever black flags waved.
I see him as he turned
In that bombed offending place,

Remorse fused with terror
In his still knowable face,
His cornered outfaced stare
Blinding in the flash.

He had gone miles away
For he drank like a fish
Nightly, naturally
Swimming towards the lure
Of warm lit-up places,
The blurred mesh and murmur
Drifting among glasses
In the gregarious smoke.
How culpable was he
That last night when he broke
Our tribe's complicity?
'Now you're supposed to be
An educated man,'
I hear him say. 'Puzzle me
The right answer to that one.'

III

I missed his funeral,
Those quiet walkers
And sideways talkers
Shoaling out of his lane
To the respectable
Purring of the hearse . . .
They move in equal pace
With the habitual
Slow consolation
Of a dawdling engine,
The line lifted, hand
Over fist, cold sunshine
On the water, the land
Banked under fog: that morning
When he took me in his boat,
The screw purling, turning

Indolent fathoms white,
I tasted freedom with him.
To get out early, haul
Steadily off the bottom,
Dispraise the catch, and smile
As you find a rhythm
Working you, slow mile by mile,
Into your proper haunt
Somewhere, well out, beyond . . .

Dawn-sniffing revenant,
Plodder through midnight rain,
Question me again.

Badgers

When the badger glimmered away
into another garden
you stood, half-lit with whiskey,
sensing you had disturbed
some soft returning.

The murdered dead,
you thought.
But could it not have been
some violent shattered boy
nosing out what got mislaid
between the cradle and the explosion,
evenings when windows stood open
and the compost smoked down the backs?

Visitations are taken for signs.
At a second house I listened
for duntings under the laurels
and heard intimations whispered
about being vaguely honoured.

And to read even by carcasses
the badgers have come back.
One that grew notorious
lay untouched in the roadside.
Last night one had me braking
but more in fear than in honour.

Cool from the sett and redolent
of his runs under the night,
the bogey of fern country
broke cover in me
for what he is:
pig family
and not at all what he's painted.

How perilous is it to choose
not to love the life we're shown?
His sturdy dirty body
and interloping grovel.
The intelligence in his bone.
The unquestionable houseboy's shoulders
that could have been my own.

The Singer's House

When they said *Carrickfergus* I could hear
the frosty echo of saltminers' picks.
I imagined it, chambered and glinting,
a township built of light.

What do we say any more
to conjure the salt of our earth?
So much comes and is gone
that should be crystal and kept,

and amicable weathers
that bring up the grain of things,
their tang of season and store,
are all the packing we'll get.

So I say to myself *Gweebarra*
and its music hits off the place
like water hitting off granite.
I see the glittering sound

framed in your window,
knives and forks set on oilcloth,
and the seals' heads, suddenly outlined,
scanning everything.

People here used to believe
that drowned souls lived in the seals.
At spring tides they might change shape.
They loved music and swam in for a singer

who might stand at the end of summer
in the mouth of a whitewashed turf-shed,
his shoulder to the jamb, his song
a rowboat far out in evening.

When I came here first you were always singing,
a hint of the clip of the pick
in your winnowing climb and attack.
Raise it again, man. We still believe what we hear.

The Guttural Muse

Late summer, and at midnight
I smelt the heat of the day:
At my window over the hotel car park
I breathed the muddied night airs off the lake
And watched a young crowd leave the discotheque.

Their voices rose up thick and comforting
As oily bubbles the feeding tench sent up
That evening at dusk—the slimy tench
Once called the 'doctor fish' because his slime
Was said to heal the wounds of fish that touched it.

A girl in a white dress
Was being courted out among the cars:
As her voice swarmed and puddled into laughs
I felt like some old pike all badged with sores
Wanting to swim in touch with soft-mouthed life.

Glanmore Sonnets

for Ann Saddlemyer
'our heartiest welcomer'

I

Vowels ploughed into other: opened ground.
The mildest February for twenty years
Is mist bands over furrows, a deep no sound
Vulnerable to distant gargling tractors.
Our road is steaming, the turned-up acres breathe.
Now the good life could be to cross a field
And art a paradigm of earth new from the lathe
Of ploughs. My lea is deeply tilled.
Old plough-socks gorge the subsoil of each sense
And I am quickened with a redolence
Of farmland as a dark unblown rose.
Wait then . . . Breasting the mist, in sowers' aprons,
My ghosts come striding into their spring stations.
The dream grain whirls like freakish Easter snows.

II

Sensings, mountings from the hiding places,
Words entering almost the sense of touch,
Ferreting themselves out of their dark hutch—
'These things are not secrets but mysteries,'
Oisin Kelly told me years ago
In Belfast, hankering after stone
That connived with the chisel, as if the grain
Remembered what the mallet tapped to know.
Then I landed in the hedge-school of Glanmore
And from the backs of ditches hoped to raise
A voice caught back off slug-horn and slow chanter
That might continue, hold, dispel, appease:
Vowels ploughed into other, opened ground,
Each verse returning like the plough turned round.

III

This evening the cuckoo and the corncrake
(So much, too much) consorted at twilight.
It was all crepuscular and iambic.
Out on the field a baby rabbit
Took his bearings, and I knew the deer
(I've seen them too from the window of the house,
Like connoisseurs, inquisitive of air)
Were careful under larch and May-green spruce.
I had said earlier, 'I won't relapse
From this strange loneliness I've brought us to.
Dorothy and William—' She interrupts:
'You're not going to compare us two . . . ?'
Outside a rustling and twig-combing breeze
Refreshes and relents. Is cadences.

IV

I used to lie with an ear to the line
For that way, they said, there should come a sound
Escaping ahead, an iron tune
Of flange and piston pitched along the ground,
But I never heard that. Always, instead,
Struck couplings and shuntings two miles away
Lifted over the woods. The head
Of a horse swirled back from a gate, a grey
Turnover of haunch and mane, and I'd look
Up to the cutting where she'd soon appear.
Two fields back, in the house, small ripples shook
Silently across our drinking water
(As they are shaking now across my heart)
And vanished into where they seemed to start.

V

Soft corrugations in the boortree's trunk,
Its green young shoots, its rods like freckled solder:
It was our bower as children, a greenish, dank
And snapping memory as I get older.
And elderberry I have learned to call it.
I love its blooms like saucers brimmed with meal,
Its berries a swart caviar of shot,
A buoyant spawn, a light bruised out of purple.
Elderberry? It is shires dreaming wine.
Boortree is bower tree, where I played 'touching tongues'
And felt another's texture quick on mine.
So, etymologist of roots and graftings,
I fall back to my tree-house and would crouch
Where small buds shoot and flourish in the hush.

VI

He lived there in the unsayable lights.
He saw the fuchsia in a drizzling noon,
The elderflower at dusk like a risen moon
And green fields greying on the windswept heights.
'I will break through,' he said, 'what I glazed over
With perfect mist and peaceful absences'—
Sudden and sure as the man who dared the ice
And raced his bike across the Moyola River.
A man we never saw. But in that winter
Of nineteen forty-seven, when the snow
Kept the country bright as a studio,
In a cold where things might crystallize or founder,
His story quickened us, a wild white goose
Heard after dark above the drifted house.

VII

Dogger, Rockall, Malin, Irish Sea:
Green, swift upsurges, North Atlantic flux
Conjured by that strong gale-warning voice,
Collapse into a sibilant penumbra.
Midnight and closedown. Sirens of the tundra,
Of eel-road, seal-road, keel-road, whale-road, raise
Their wind-compounded keen behind the baize
And drive the trawlers to the lee of Wicklow.
L'Etoile, Le Guillemot, La Belle Hélène
Nursed their bright names this morning in the bay
That toiled like mortar. It was marvellous
And actual, I said out loud, 'A haven,'
The word deepening, clearing, like the sky
Elsewhere on Minches, Cromarty, The Faroes.

VIII

Thunderlight on the split logs: big raindrops
At body heat and lush with omen
Spattering dark on the hatchet iron.
This morning when a magpie with jerky steps
Inspected a horse asleep beside the wood
I thought of dew on armour and carrion.
What would I meet, blood-boltered, on the road?
How deep into the woodpile sat the toad?
What welters through this dark hush on the crops?
Do you remember that *pension* in Les Landes
Where the old one rocked and rocked and rocked
A mongol in her lap, to little songs?
Come to me quick, I am upstairs shaking.
My all of you birchwood in lightning.

IX

Outside the kitchen window a black rat
Sways on the briar like infected fruit:
'It looked me through, it stared me out, I'm not
Imagining things. Go you out to it.'
Did we come to the wilderness for this?
We have our burnished bay tree at the gate,
Classical, hung with the reek of silage
From the next farm, tart-leafed as inwit.
Blood on a pitchfork, blood on chaff and hay,
Rats speared in the sweat and dust of threshing—
What is my apology for poetry?
The empty briar is swishing
When I come down, and beyond, inside, your face
Haunts like a new moon glimpsed through tangled glass.

X

I dreamt we slept in a moss in Donegal
On turf banks under blankets, with our faces
Exposed all night in a wetting drizzle,
Pallid as the dripping sapling birches.
Lorenzo and Jessica in a cold climate.
Diarmuid and Grainne waiting to be found.
Darkly asperged and censed, we were laid out
Like breathing effigies on a raised ground.
And in that dream I dreamt—how like you this?—
Our first night years ago in that hotel
When you came with your deliberate kiss
To raise us towards the lovely and painful
Covenants of flesh; our separateness;
The respite in our dewy dreaming faces.

An Afterwards

She would plunge all poets in the ninth circle
And fix them, tooth in skull, tonguing for brain;
For backbiting in life she'd make their hell
A rabid egotistical daisy-chain.

Unyielding, spurred, ambitious, unblunted,
Lockjawed, mantrapped, each a fastened badger
Jockeying for position, hasped and mounted
Like Ugolino on Archbishop Roger.

And when she'd make her circuit of the ice,
Aided and abetted by Virgil's wife,
I would cry out, 'My sweet, who wears the bays
In our green land above, whose is the life

Most dedicated and exemplary?'
And she: 'I have closed my widowed ears
To the sulphurous news of poets and poetry.
Why could you not have, oftener, in our years

Unclenched, and come down laughing from your room
And walked the twilight with me and your children—
Like that one evening of elder bloom
And hay, when the wild roses were fading?'

And (as some maker gaffs me in the neck)
'You weren't the worst. You aspired to a kind,
Indifferent, faults-on-both-sides tact.
You first left us, and then those books, behind.'

The Otter

When you plunged
The light of Tuscany wavered
And swung through the pool
From top to bottom.

I loved your wet head and smashing crawl,
Your fine swimmer's back and shoulders
Surfacing and surfacing again
This year and every year since.

I sat dry-throated on the warm stones.
You were beyond me.
The mellowed clarities, the grape-deep air
Thinned and disappointed.

Thank God for the slow loadening:
When I hold you now
We are close and deep
As the atmosphere on water.

My two hands are plumbed water.
You are my palpable, lithe
Otter of memory
In the pool of the moment,

Turning to swim on your back,
Each silent, thigh-shaking kick
Retilting the light,
Heaving the cool at your neck.

And suddenly you're out,
Back again, intent as ever,
Heavy and frisky in your freshened pelt,
Printing the stones.

The Skunk

Up, black, striped and damasked like the chasuble
At a funeral Mass, the skunk's tail
Paraded the skunk. Night after night
I expected her like a visitor.

The refrigerator whinnied into silence.
My desk light softened beyond the verandah.
Small oranges loomed in the orange tree.
I began to be tense as a voyeur.

After eleven years I was composing
Love-letters again, broaching the word 'wife'
Like a stored cask, as if its slender vowel
Had mutated into the night earth and air

Of California. The beautiful, useless
Tang of eucalyptus spelt your absence.
The aftermath of a mouthful of wine
Was like inhaling you off a cold pillow.

And there she was, the intent and glamorous,
Ordinary, mysterious skunk,
Mythologized, demythologized,
Snuffing the boards five feet beyond me.

It all came back to me last night, stirred
By the sootfall of your things at bedtime,
Your head-down, tail-up hunt in a bottom drawer
For the black plunge-line nightdress.

A Dream of Jealousy

Walking with you and another lady
In wooded parkland, the whispering grass
Ran its fingers through our guessing silence
And the trees opened into a shady
Unexpected clearing where we sat down.
I think the candour of the light dismayed us.
We talked about desire and being jealous,
Our conversation a loose single gown
Or a white picnic tablecloth spread out
Like a book of manners in the wilderness.
'Show me,' I said to our companion, 'what
I have much coveted, your breast's mauve star.'
And she consented. Oh neither these verses
Nor my prudence, love, can heal your wounded stare.

Field Work

I

Where the sally tree went pale in every breeze,
where the perfect eye of the nesting blackbird watched,
where one fern was always green

I was standing watching you
take the pad from the gatehouse at the crossing
and reach to lift a white wash off the whins.

I could see the vaccination mark
stretched on your upper arm, and smell the coal smell
of the train that comes between us, a slow goods,

waggon after waggon full of big-eyed cattle.

II

But your vaccination mark is on your thigh,
an O that's healed into the bark.

Except a dryad's not a woman
you are my wounded dryad

in a mothering smell of wet
and ring-wormed chestnuts.

Our moon was small and far,
was a coin long gazed at

brilliant on the *Pequod*'s mast
across Atlantic and Pacific waters.

III

Not the mud slick,
not the black weedy water
full of alder cones and pock-marked leaves.

Not the cow parsley in winter
with its old whitened shins and wrists,
its sibilance, its shaking.

Not even the tart green shade of summer
thick with butterflies
and fungus plump as a leather saddle.

No. But in a still corner,
braced to its pebble-dashed wall,
heavy, earth-drawn, all mouth and eye,

the sunflower, dreaming umber.

IV

Catspiss smell,
the pink bloom open:
I press a leaf
of the flowering currant
on the back of your hand
for the tight slow burn
of its sticky juice
to prime your skin,
and your veins to be crossed
criss-cross with leaf-veins.
I lick my thumb
and dip it in mould,
I anoint the anointed
leaf-shape. Mould
blooms and pigments
the back of your hand
like a birthmark—

my umber one,
you are stained, stained
to perfection.

Song

A rowan like a lipsticked girl.
Between the by-road and the main road
Alder trees at a wet and dripping distance
Stand off among the rushes.

There are the mud-flowers of dialect
And the immortelles of perfect pitch
And that moment when the bird sings very close
To the music of what happens.

Leavings

A soft whoosh, the sunset blaze
of straw on blackened stubble,
a thatch-deep, freshening
barbarous crimson burn—

I rode down England
as they fired the crop
that was the leavings of a crop,
the smashed tow-coloured barley,

down from Ely's Lady Chapel,
the sweet tenor Latin
forever banished,
the sumptuous windows

threshed clear by Thomas Cromwell.
Which circle does he tread,
scalding on cobbles,
each one a broken statue's head?

After midnight, after summer,
to walk in a sparking field,
to smell dew and ashes
and start Will Brangwen's ghost

from the hot soot—
a breaking sheaf of light,
abroad in the hiss
and clash of stooking.

The Harvest Bow

As you plaited the harvest bow
You implicated the mellowed silence in you
In wheat that does not rust
But brightens as it tightens twist by twist
Into a knowable corona,
A throwaway love-knot of straw.

Hands that aged round ashplants and cane sticks
And lapped the spurs on a lifetime of gamecocks
Harked to their gift and worked with fine intent
Until your fingers moved somnambulant:
I tell and finger it like braille,
Gleaning the unsaid off the palpable.

And if I spy into its golden loops
I see us walk between the railway slopes
Into an evening of long grass and midges,
Blue smoke straight up, old beds and ploughs in hedges,
An auction notice on an outhouse wall—
You with a harvest bow in your lapel,

Me with the fishing rod, already homesick
For the big lift of these evenings, as your stick
Whacking the tips off weeds and bushes
Beats out of time, and beats, but flushes
Nothing: that original townland
Still tongue-tied in the straw tied by your hand.

The end of art is peace
Could be the motto of this frail device
That I have pinned up on our deal dresser—
Like a drawn snare
Slipped lately by the spirit of the corn
Yet burnished by its passage, and still warm.

In Memoriam Francis Ledwidge

killed in France 31 July 1917

The bronze soldier hitches a bronze cape
That crumples stiffly in imagined wind
No matter how the real winds buff and sweep
His sudden hunkering run, forever craned

Over Flanders. Helmet and haversack,
The gun's firm slope from butt to bayonet,
The loyal, fallen names on the embossed plaque—
It all meant little to the worried pet

I was in nineteen forty-six or -seven,
Gripping my Aunt Mary by the hand
Along the Portstewart prom, then round the crescent
To thread the Castle Walk out to the strand.

The pilot from Coleraine sailed to the coal-boat.
Courting couples rose out of the dunes.
A farmer stripped to his studs and shiny waistcoat
Rolled the trousers down on his timid shins.

Francis Ledwidge, you courted at the seaside
Beyond Drogheda one Sunday afternoon.
Literary, sweet-talking, countrified,
You pedalled out the leafy road from Slane

Where you belonged, among the dolorous
And lovely: the May altar of wild flowers,
Easter water sprinkled in outhouses,
Mass-rocks and hill-top raths and raftered byres.

I think of you in your Tommy's uniform,
A haunted Catholic face, pallid and brave,
Ghosting the trenches like a bloom of hawthorn
Or silence cored from a Boyne passage-grave.

It's summer, nineteen-fifteen. I see the girl
My aunt was then, herding on the long acre.
Behind a low bush in the Dardanelles
You suck stones to make your dry mouth water.

It's nineteen-seventeen. She still herds cows
But a big strafe puts the candles out in Ypres:
'My soul is by the Boyne, cutting new meadows . . .
My country wears her confirmation dress.'

'To be called a British soldier while my country
Has no place among nations . . .' You were rent
By shrapnel six weeks later. 'I am sorry
That party politics should divide our tents.'

In you, our dead enigma, all the strains
Criss-cross in useless equilibrium
And as the wind tunes through this vigilant bronze
I hear again the sure confusing drum

You followed from Boyne water to the Balkans
But miss the twilit note your flute should sound.
You were not keyed or pitched like these true-blue ones
Though all of you consort now underground.

Ugolino

(*from* D A N T E , *Inferno*, XXXII, XXXIII)

We had already left him. I walked the ice
And saw two soldered in a frozen hole
On top of other, one's skull capping the other's,
Gnawing at him where the neck and head
Are grafted to the sweet fruit of the brain,
Like a famine victim at a loaf of bread.
So the berserk Tydeus gnashed and fed
Upon the severed head of Menalippus
As if it were some spattered carnal melon.
'You,' I shouted, 'you on top, what hate
Makes you so ravenous and insatiable?
What keeps you so monstrously at rut?
Is there any story I can tell
For you, in the world above, against him?
If my tongue by then's not withered in my throat
I will report the truth and clear your name.'

That sinner eased his mouth up off his meal
To answer me, and wiped it with the hair
Left growing on his victim's ravaged skull,
Then said, 'Even before I speak
The thought of having to relive all that
Desperate time makes my heart sick;
Yet while I weep to say them, I would sow
My words like curses—that they might increase
And multiply upon this head I gnaw.
I know you come from Florence by your accent
But I have no idea who you are
Or how you ever managed your descent.
Still, you should know my name, for I was Count
Ugolino, this was Archbishop Roger,
And why I act the jockey to his mount
Is surely common knowledge; how my good faith
Was easy prey to his malignancy,

How I was taken, held, and put to death.
But you must hear something you cannot know
If you're to judge him—the cruelty
Of my death at his hands. So listen now.

Others will pine as I pined in that jail
Which is called Hunger after me, and watch
As I watched through a narrow hole
Moon after moon, bright and somnambulant,
Pass overhead, until that night I dreamt
The bad dream and my future's veil was rent.
I saw a wolf-hunt: this man rode the hill
Between Pisa and Lucca, hounding down
The wolf and wolf-cubs. He was lordly and masterful,
His pack in keen condition, his company
Deployed ahead of him, Gualandi
And Sismundi as well, and Lanfranchi,
Who soon wore down wolf-father and wolf-sons
And my hallucination
Was all sharp teeth and bleeding flanks ripped open.
When I awoke before the dawn, my head
Swam with cries of my sons who slept in tears
Beside me there, crying out for bread.
(If your sympathy has not already started
At all that my heart was foresuffering
And if you are not crying, you are hardhearted.)

They were awake now, it was near the time
For food to be brought in as usual,
Each one of them disturbed after his dream,
When I heard the door being nailed and hammered
Shut, far down in the nightmare tower.
I stared in my sons' faces and spoke no word.
My eyes were dry and my heart was stony.
They cried and my little Anselm said,
"What is wrong? Why are you staring, Daddy?"
But I shed no tears, I made no reply
All through that day, all through the night that followed
Until another sun blushed in the sky

And sent a small beam probing the distress
Inside those prison walls. Then when I saw
The image of my face in their four faces
I bit on my two hands in desperation
And they, since they thought hunger drove me to it,
Rose up suddenly in agitation
Saying, "Father, it will greatly ease our pain
If you eat us instead, and you who dressed us
In this sad flesh undress us here again."
So then I calmed myself to keep them calm.
We hushed. That day and the next stole past us
And earth seemed hardened against me and them.
For four days we let the silence gather.
Then, throwing himself flat in front of me,
Gaddo said, "Why don't you help me, Father?"
He died like that, and as surely as you see
Me here, one by one I saw my three
Drop dead during the fifth day and the sixth day
Until I saw no more. Searching, blinded,
For two days I groped over them and called them.
Then hunger killed where grief had only wounded.'
When he had said all this, his eyes rolled
And his teeth, like a dog's teeth clamping round a bone,
Bit into the skull and again took hold.

Pisa! Pisa, your sounds are like a hiss
Sizzling in our country's grassy language.
And since the neighbour states have been remiss
In your extermination, let a huge
Dyke of islands bar the Arno's mouth, let
Capraia and Gorgona dam and deluge
You and your population. For the sins
Of Ugolino, who betrayed your forts,
Should never have been visited on his sons.
Your atrocity was Theban. They were young
And innocent: Hugh and Brigata
And the other two whose names are in my song.

FROM

Sweeney Astray

[1 9 8 3]

Sweeney in Flight

When Sweeney heard the shouts of the soldiers and the big noise
of the army, he rose out of the tree towards the dark clouds and
ranged far over mountains and territories.

A long time he went faring all through Ireland,
poking his way into hard rocky clefts,
shouldering through ivy bushes,
unsettling falls of pebbles in narrow defiles,
wading estuaries,
breasting summits,
trekking through glens,
until he found the pleasures of Glen Bolcain.

That place is a natural asylum where all the madmen of Ireland
used to assemble once their year in madness was complete.

Glen Bolcain is like this:
it has four gaps to the wind,
pleasant woods, clean-banked wells,
cold springs and clear sandy streams
where green-topped watercress and languid brooklime
philander over the surface.
It is nature's pantry
with its sorrels, its wood-sorrels,
its berries, its wild garlic,
its black sloes and its brown acorns.

The madmen would beat each other for the pick of its water-
cresses and for the beds on its banks.

Sweeney stayed a long time in that glen until one night he was
cooped up in the top of a tall ivy-grown hawthorn. He could
hardly endure it, for every time he twisted or turned, the thorny
twigs would flail him so that he was prickled and cut and bleed-

ing all over. He changed from that station to another one, a clump of thick briars with a single young blackthorn standing up out of the thorny bed, and he settled in the top of the blackthorn. But it was too slender. It wobbled and bent so that Sweeney fell heavily through the thicket and ended up on the ground like a man in a bloodbath. Then he gathered himself up, exhausted and beaten, and came out of the thicket, saying:

—It is hard to bear this life after the pleasant times I knew. And it has been like this a year to the night last night!

Then he spoke this poem:

A year until last night
I have lived among dark trees,
between the flood and ebb-tide,
going cold and naked

with no pillow for my head,
no human company
and, so help me, God,
no spear and no sword!

No sweet talk with women.
Instead, I pine
for cresses, for the clean
pickings of brooklime.

No surge of royal blood,
camped here in solitude;
no glory flames the wood,
no friends, no music.

Tell the truth: a hard lot.
And no shirking this fate;
no sleep, no respite,
no hope for a long time.

No house humming full,
no men, loud with good will,
nobody to call me king,
no drink or banqueting.

A great gulf yawns now
between me and my retinue,
between craziness and reason.
Scavenging through the glen

on my mad king's visit:
no pomp or poet's circuit
but wild scuttles in the wood.
Heavenly saints! O Holy God!

No skilled musicians' cunning,
no soft discoursing women,
no open-handed giving;
my doom to be a long dying.

Our sorrows were multiplied
that Tuesday when Congal fell.
Our dead made a great harvest,
our remnant, a last swathe.

This has been my plight.
Suddenly cast out,
grieving and astray,
a year until last night.

Sweeney kept going until he reached the church at Swim-Two-
Birds on the Shannon, which is now called Cloonburren; he ar-
rived there on a Friday, to be exact. The clerics of the church
were singing nones, women were beating flax and one was giv-
ing birth to a child.

    —It is unseemly, said Sweeney, for the women to violate
the Lord's fast day. That woman beating the flax reminds me
of our beating at Moira.

    Then he heard the vesper bell ringing and said:

    —It would be sweeter to listen to the notes of the cuckoos
on the banks of the Bann than to the whinge of this bell tonight.

    Then he uttered the poem:

I perched for rest and imagined
cuckoos calling across water,

the Bann cuckoo, calling sweeter
than church bells that whinge and grind.

Friday is the wrong day, woman,
for you to give birth to a son,
the day when mad Sweeney fasts
for love of God, in penitence.

Do not just discount me. Listen.
At Moira my tribe was beaten,
beetled, heckled, hammered down,
like flax being scutched by these women.

From the cliff of Lough Diolar
up to Derry Colmcille
I saw the great swans, heard their calls
sweetly rebuking wars and battles.

From lonely cliff-tops, the stag
bells and makes the whole glen shake
and re-echo. I am ravished.
Unearthly sweetness shakes my breast.

O Christ, the loving and the sinless,
hear my prayer, attend, O Christ,
and let nothing separate us.
Blend me forever in your sweetness.

It was the end of the harvest season and Sweeney heard a
hunting-call from a company in the skirts of the wood.

—This will be the outcry of the Ui Faolain coming to kill
me, he said. I slew their king at Moira and this host is out to
avenge him.

He heard the stag bellowing and he made a poem in which
he praised aloud all the trees of Ireland, and rehearsed some of
his own hardships and sorrows, saying:

The bushy leafy oak tree
is highest in the wood,
the forking shoots of hazel
hide sweet hazel-nuts.

The alder is my darling,
all thornless in the gap,
some milk of human kindness
coursing in its sap.

The blackthorn is a jaggy creel
stippled with dark sloes;
green watercress in thatch on wells
where the drinking blackbird goes.

Sweetest of the leafy stalks,
the vetches strew the pathway;
the oyster-grass is my delight,
and the wild strawberry.

Low-set clumps of apple trees
drum down fruit when shaken;
scarlet berries clot like blood
on mountain rowan.

Briars curl in sideways,
arch a stickle back,
draw blood and curl up innocent
to sneak the next attack.

The yew tree in each churchyard
wraps night in its dark hood.
Ivy is a shadowy
genius of the wood.

Holly rears its windbreak,
a door in winter's face;
life-blood on a spear-shaft
darkens the grain of ash.

Birch tree, smooth and blessed,
delicious to the breeze,
high twigs plait and crown it
the queen of trees.

The aspen pales
and whispers, hesitates:
a thousand frightened scuts
race in its leaves.

But what disturbs me most
in the leafy wood
is the to and fro and to and fro
of an oak rod.

*

A starry frost will come
dropping on the pools
and I'll be astray
on unsheltered heights:

herons calling
in cold Glenelly,
flocks of birds quickly
coming and going.

I prefer the elusive
rhapsody of blackbirds
to the garrulous blather
of men and women.

I prefer the squeal of badgers
in their sett
to the tally-ho
of the morning hunt.

I prefer the re-
echoing belling of a stag
among the peaks
to that arrogant horn.

Those unharnessed runners
from glen to glen!
Nobody tames
that royal blood,

each one aloof
on its rightful summit,
antlered, watchful.
Imagine them,

the stag of high Slieve Felim,
the stag of the steep Fews,
the stag of Duhallow, the stag of Orrery,
the fierce stag of Killarney.

The stag of Islandmagee, Larne's stag,
the stag of Moylinny,
the stag of Cooley, the stag of Cunghill,
the stag of the two-peaked Burren.

*

I am Sweeney, the whinger,
the scuttler in the valley.
But call me, instead,
Peak-pate, Stag-head.

Then Sweeney said:
— From now on, I won't tarry in Dal-Arie because Lynch-
seachan would have my life to avenge the hag's.
So he proceeded to Roscommon in Connacht, where he
alighted on the bank of the well and treated himself to water-
cress and water. But when a woman came out of the erenach's
house, he panicked and fled, and she gathered the watercress
from the stream. Sweeney watched her from his tree and greatly
lamented the theft of his patch of cress, saying:
— It is a shame that you are taking my watercress. If only
you knew my plight, how I am unpitied by tribesman or kins-
man, how I am no longer a guest in any house on the ridge of
the world. Watercress is my wealth, water is my wine, and hard
bare trees and soft tree bowers are my friends. Even if you left

that cress, you would not be left wanting; but if you take it, you
are taking the bite from my mouth.
  And he made this poem:

Woman, picking the watercress
and scooping up my drink of water,
were you to leave them as my due
you would still be none the poorer.

Woman, have consideration,
we two go two different ways:
I perch out among the tree-tops,
you lodge in a friendly house.

Woman, have consideration.
Think of me in the sharp wind,
forgotten, past consideration,
shivering, stripped to the skin.

Woman, you cannot start to know
sorrows Sweeney has forgotten:
how friends were so long denied him
he killed his gift for friendship even.

Fugitive, deserted, mocked
by memories of his days as king,
no longer called to head the troop
when warriors are mustering,

no longer an honoured guest
at tables anywhere in Ireland,
ranging like a mad pilgrim
over rock-peaks on the mountain.

The harper who harped me to rest,
where is his soothing music now?
My people too, my kith and kin,
where did their affection go?

In my heyday, I, on horseback,
came riding high into my own:
now memory's an unbroken horse
that rears and suddenly throws me down.

Over starlit moors and plains,
woman plucking my watercress,
to his cold and lonely station
the shadow of that Sweeney goes

with watercresses for his herds,
cold water for his mead,
bushes for companions,
the bare hillside for his bed.

Gazing down at clean gravel,
to lean out over a cool well,
drink a mouthful of sunlit water
and gather cresses by the handful—

even this you would pluck from me,
lean pickings that have thinned my blood
and chilled me on the cold uplands,
hunkering low when winds spring up.

Morning wind is the coldest wind,
it flays me of my rags, it freezes—
the very memory leaves me speechless,
woman, picking the watercress.

He stayed in Roscommon that night and the next day he went
on to Slieve Aughty, from there to the pleasant slopes of Slem-
ish, then on to the high peaks of Slieve Bloom, and from there
to Inishmurray. After that, he stayed six weeks in a cave that
belonged to Donnan on the island of Eig off the west of Scot-
land. From there he went on to Ailsa Craig, where he spent
another six weeks, and when he finally left he bade the place
farewell and bewailed his state, like this:

Without bed or board
I face dark days
in frozen lairs
and wind-driven snow.

Ice scoured by winds.
Watery shadows from weak sun.
Shelter from the one tree
on a plateau.

Haunting deer-paths,
enduring rain,
first-footing the grey
frosted grass.

I climb towards the pass
and the stag's belling
rings off the wood,
surf-noise rises

where I go, heartbroken
and worn out,
sharp-haunched Sweeney,
raving and moaning.

The sough of the winter night,
my feet packing the hailstones
as I pad the dappled
banks of Mourne

or lie, unslept, in a wet bed
on the hills by Lough Erne,
tensed for first light
and an early start.

Skimming the waves
at Dunseverick,
listening to billows
at Dun Rodairce,

hurtling from that great wave
to the wave running
in tidal Barrow,
one night in hard Dun Cernan,

the next among the wild flowers
of Benn Boirne;
and then a stone pillow
on the screes of Croagh Patrick.

*

But to have ended up
lamenting here
on Ailsa Craig.
A hard station!

Ailsa Craig,
the seagulls' home,
God knows
it is hard lodgings.

Ailsa Craig,
bell-shaped rock,
reaching sky-high,
snout in the sea—

it hard-beaked,
me skimped and scraggy:
we mated like a couple
of hard-shanked cranes.

Once when Sweeney was rambling and raking through Connacht he ended up in Alternan in Tireragh. A community of holy people had made their home there, and it was a lovely valley, with a turbulent river shooting down the cliff; trees fruited and blossomed on the cliff face; there were sheltering ivies and heavy-topped orchards, there were wild deer and hares and fat swine; and sleek seals, that used to sleep on the cliff, having come in from the ocean beyond. Sweeney coveted the place mightily and sang its praises aloud in this poem:

Sainted cliff at Alternan,
nut grove, hazel-wood!
Cold quick sweeps of water
fall down the cliff-side.

Ivies green and thicken there,
its oak-mast is precious.
Fruited branches nod and bend
from heavy-headed apple trees.

Badgers make their setts there
and swift hares have their form;
and seals' heads swim the ocean,
cobbling the running foam.

And by the waterfall, Colman's son,
haggard, spent, frost-bitten Sweeney,
Ronan of Drumgesh's victim,
is sleeping at the foot of a tree.

At last Sweeney arrived where Moling lived, the place that is known as St Mullins. Just then, Moling was addressing himself to Kevin's psalter and reading from it to his students. Sweeney presented himself at the brink of the well and began to eat watercress.

—You are more than welcome here, Sweeney, said Moling, for you are fated to live and die here. You shall leave the history of your adventures with us and receive a Christian burial in a churchyard. Therefore, said Moling, no matter how far you range over Ireland, day by day, I bind you to return to me every evening so that I may record your story.

All during the next year the madman kept coming back to Moling. One day he would go to Inishbofin in west Connacht, another day to lovely Assaroe. Some days he would view the clean lines of Slemish, some days he would be shivering on the Mournes. But wherever he went, every night he would be back for vespers at St Mullins.

Moling ordered his cook to leave aside some of each day's

milking for Sweeney's supper. This cook's name was Muirghil and she was married to a swineherd of Moling's called Mongan. Anyhow, Sweeney's supper was like this: she would sink her heel to the ankle in the nearest cow-dung and fill the hole to the brim with new milk. Then Sweeney would sneak into the deserted corner of the milking yard and lap it up.

One night there was a row between Muirghil and another woman, in the course of which the woman said:

—If you do not prefer your husband, it is a pity you cannot take up with some other man than the looney you have been meeting all year.

The herd's sister was within earshot and listening, but she said nothing until the next morning. Then when she saw Muirghil going to leave the milk in the cow-dung beside the hedge where Sweeney roosted, she came in to her brother and said:

—Are you a man at all? Your wife's down yonder in the hedge with somebody else.

Jealousy shook him like a brainstorm. He got up in a sudden fury, seized a spear from a rack in the house, and made for the madman. Sweeney was down swilling the milk out of the cow-dung with his side exposed towards the herd, who let go at him with the spear. It went into Sweeney at the nipple of his left breast, went through him, and broke his back.

There is another story. Some say the herd had hidden a deer's horn at the spot where Sweeney drank from the cow-dung and that Sweeney fell and killed himself on the point of it.

Immediately, Moling and his community came along to where Sweeney lay and Sweeney repented and made his confession to Moling. He received Christ's body and thanked God for having received it and after that was anointed by the clerics.

There was a time when I preferred
the turtle-dove's soft jubilation
as it flitted round a pool
to the murmur of conversation.

There was a time when I preferred
the blackbird singing on the hill

and the stag loud against the storm
to the clinking tongue of this bell.

There was a time when I preferred
the mountain grouse crying at dawn
to the voice and closeness
of a beautiful woman.

There was a time when I preferred
wolf-packs yelping and howling
to the sheepish voice of a cleric
bleating out plainsong.

You are welcome to pledge healths
and carouse in your drinking dens;
I will dip and steal water
from a well with my open palm.

You are welcome to that cloistered hush
of your students' conversation;
I will study the pure chant
of hounds baying in Glen Bolcain.

You are welcome to your salt meat
and fresh meat in feasting-houses;
I will live content elsewhere
on tufts of green watercress.

The herd's sharp spear has finished me,
passed clean through my body.
Ah Christ, who disposes all things, why
was I not killed at Moira?

Then Sweeney's death-swoon came over him and Moling, at-
tended by his clerics, rose up and each of them placed a stone
on Sweeney's grave.

The Names of the Hare

(from the Middle English)

The man the hare has met
will never be the better for it
except he lay down on the land
what he carries in his hand—
be it staff or be it bow—
and bless him with his elbow
and come out with this litany
with devotion and sincerity
to speak the praises of the hare.
Then the man will better fare.

'The hare, call him scotart,
big-fellow, bouchart,
the O'Hare, the jumper,
the rascal, the racer.

Beat-the-pad, white-face,
funk-the-ditch, shit-ass.

The wimount, the messer,
the skidaddler, the nibbler,
the ill-met, the slabber.

The quick-scut, the dew-flirt,
the grass-biter, the goibert,
the home-late, the do-the-dirt.

The starer, the wood-cat,
the purblind, the furze cat,
the skulker, the bleary-eyed,
the wall-eyed, the glance-aside
and also the hedge-springer.

The stubble-stag, the long lugs,
the stook-deer, the frisky legs,
the wild one, the skipper,
the hug-the-ground, the lurker,
the race-the-wind, the skiver,
the shag-the-hare, the hedge-squatter,
the dew-hammer, the dew-hopper,
the sit-tight, the grass-bounder,
the jig-foot, the earth-sitter,
the light-foot, the fern-sitter,
the kail-stag, the herb-cropper.

The creep-along, the sitter-still,
the pintail, the ring-the-hill,
the sudden start,
the shake-the-heart,
the belly-white,
the lambs-in-flight.

The gobshite, the gum-sucker,
the scare-the-man, the faith-breaker,
the snuff-the-ground, the baldy skull
(his chief name is scoundrel).

The stag sprouting a suede horn,
the creature living in the corn,
the creature bearing all men's scorn,
the creature no one dares to name.'

When you have got all this said
then the hare's strength has been laid.
Then you might go faring forth—
east and west and south and north,
wherever you incline to go—
but only if you're skilful too.
And now, Sir Hare, good-day to you.
God guide you to a how-d'ye-do
with me: come to me dead
in either onion broth or bread.

FROM

Station Island

[1 9 8 4]

The Underground

There we were in the vaulted tunnel running,
You in your going-away coat speeding ahead
And me, me then like a fleet god gaining
Upon you before you turned to a reed

Or some new white flower japped with crimson
As the coat flapped wild and button after button
Sprang off and fell in a trail
Between the Underground and the Albert Hall.

Honeymooning, mooning around, late for the Proms,
Our echoes die in that corridor and now
I come as Hansel came on the moonlit stones
Retracing the path back, lifting the buttons

To end up in a draughty lamplit station
After the trains have gone, the wet track
Bared and tensed as I am, all attention
For your step following and damned if I look back.

Sloe Gin

The clear weather of juniper
darkened into winter.
She fed gin to sloes
and sealed the glass container.

When I unscrewed it
I smelled the disturbed
tart stillness of a bush
rising through the pantry.

When I poured it
it had a cutting edge
and flamed
like Betelgeuse.

I drink to you
in smoke-mirled, blue-
black sloes, bitter
and dependable.

Chekhov on Sakhalin

for Derek Mahon

So, he would pay his 'debt to medicine'.
But first he drank cognac by the ocean
With his back to all he had travelled there to face.
His head was swimming free as the troikas

Of Tyumen, he looked down from the rail
Of his thirty years and saw a mile
Into himself as if he were clear water:
Lake Baikal from the deckrail of the steamer.

So far away, Moscow was like lost youth.
And who was he, to savour in his mouth
Fine spirits that the puzzled literati
Packed off with him to a penal colony—

Him, born, you may say, under the counter?
At least that meant he knew its worth. No cantor
In full throat by the iconostasis
Got holier joy than he got from that glass

That shone and warmed like diamonds warming
On some pert young cleavage in a salon,
Inviolable and affronting.
He felt the glass go cold in the midnight sun.

When he staggered up and smashed it on the stones
It rang as clearly as the convicts' chains
That haunted him. All through the months to come
It rang on like the burden of his freedom

To try for the right tone—not tract, not thesis—
And walk away from floggings. He who thought to squeeze
His slave's blood out and waken the free man
Shadowed a convict guide through Sakhalin.

Sandstone Keepsake

It is a kind of chalky russet
solidified gourd, sedimentary
and so reliably dense and bricky
I often clasp it and throw it from hand to hand.

It was ruddier, with an underwater
hint of contusion, when I lifted it,
wading a shingle beach on Inishowen.
Across the estuary light after light

came on silently round the perimeter
of the camp. A stone from Phlegethon,
bloodied on the bed of hell's hot river?
Evening frost and the salt water

made my hand smoke, as if I'd plucked the heart
that damned Guy de Montfort to the boiling flood—
but not really, though I remembered
his victim's heart in its casket, long venerated.

Anyhow, there I was with the wet red stone
in my hand, staring across at the watch-towers
from my free state of image and allusion,
swooped on, then dropped by trained binoculars:

a silhouette not worth bothering about,
out for the evening in scarf and waders
and not about to set times wrong or right,
stooping along, one of the venerators.

from *Shelf Life*

Granite Chip

Houndstooth stone. Aberdeen of the mind.

Saying *An union in the cup I'll throw*
I have hurt my hand, pressing it hard around
this bit hammered off Joyce's Martello
Tower, this flecked insoluble brilliant

I keep but feel little in common with—
a kind of stone-age circumcising knife,
a Calvin edge in my complaisant pith.
Granite is jaggy, salty, punitive

and exacting. *Come to me*, it says
*all you who labour and are burdened, I
will not refresh you.* And it adds, *Seize
the day.* And, *You can take me or leave me.*

Old Smoothing Iron

Often I watched her lift it
from where its compact wedge
rode the back of the stove
like a tug at anchor.

To test its heat she'd stare
and spit in its iron face
or hold it up next her cheek
to divine the stored danger.

Soft thumps on the ironing board.
Her dimpled angled elbow
and intent stoop
as she aimed the smoothing iron

like a plane into linen,
like the resentment of women.
To work, her dumb lunge says,
is to move a certain mass

through a certain distance,
is to pull your weight and feel
exact and equal to it.
Feel dragged upon. And buoyant.

Stone from Delphi

To be carried back to the shrine some dawn
when the sea spreads its far sun-crops to the south
and I make a morning offering again:
that I may escape the miasma of spilled blood,
govern the tongue, fear hybris, fear the god
until he speaks in my untrammelled mouth.

Making Strange

I stood between them,
the one with his travelled intelligence
and tawny containment,
his speech like the twang of a bowstring,

and another, unshorn and bewildered
in the tubs of his wellingtons,
smiling at me for help,
faced with this stranger I'd brought him.

Then a cunning middle voice
came out of the field across the road
saying, 'Be adept and be dialect,
tell of this wind coming past the zinc hut,

call me sweetbriar after the rain
or snowberries cooled in the fog.
But love the cut of this travelled one
and call me also the cornfield of Boaz.

Go beyond what's reliable
in all that keeps pleading and pleading,
these eyes and puddles and stones,
and recollect how bold you were

when I visited you first
with departures you cannot go back on.'
A chaffinch flicked from an ash and next thing
I found myself driving the stranger

through my own country, adept
at dialect, reciting my pride
in all that I knew, that began to make strange
at that same recitation.

The Birthplace

The deal table where he wrote, so small and plain,
the single bed a dream of discipline.
And a flagged kitchen downstairs, its mote-slants

of thick light: the unperturbed, reliable
ghost life he carried, with no need to invent.
And high trees round the house, breathed upon

day and night by winds as slow as a cart
coming late from market, or the stir
a fiddle could make in his reluctant heart.

II

That day, we were like one
of his troubled couples, speechless
until he spoke for them,

haunters of silence at noon
in a deep lane that was sexual
with ferns and butterflies,

scared at our hurt,
throat-sick, heat-struck, driven
into the damp-floored wood

where we made an episode
of ourselves, unforgettable,
unmentionable,

and broke out again like cattle
through bushes, wet and raised,
only yards from the house.

III

Everywhere being nowhere,
who can prove
one place more than another?

We come back emptied,
to nourish and resist
the words of coming to rest:

birthplace, roofbeam, whitewash,
flagstone, hearth,
like unstacked iron weights

afloat among galaxies.
Still, was it thirty years ago
I read until first light

for the first time, to finish
The Return of the Native?
The corncrake in the aftergrass

verified himself, and I heard
roosters and dogs, the very same
as if he had written them.

Changes

As you came with me in silence
to the pump in the long grass

I heard much that you could not hear:
the bite of the spade that sank it,

the slithering and grumble
as the mason mixed his mortar,

and women coming with white buckets
like flashes on their ruffled wings.

The cast-iron rims of the lid
clinked as I uncovered it,

something stirred in its mouth.
I had a bird's eye view of a bird,

finch-green, speckly white,
nesting on dry leaves, flattened, still,

suffering the light.
So I roofed the citadel

as gently as I could, and told you
and you gently unroofed it

but where was the bird now?
There was a single egg, pebbly white,

and in the rusted bend of the spout
tail feathers splayed and sat tight.

So tender, I said, 'Remember this.
It will be good for you to retrace this path

when you have grown away and stand at last
at the very centre of the empty city.'

A Bat on the Road

*A batlike soul waking to consciousness of itself in darkness
and secrecy and loneliness.*

You would hoist an old hat on the tines of a fork
and trawl the mouth of the bridge for the slight
bat-thump and flutter. Skinny downy webs,

babynails clawing the sweatband . . . But don't
bring it down, don't break its flight again,
don't deny it; this time let it go free.

Follow its bat-flap under the stone bridge,
under the Midland and Scottish Railway
and lose it there in the dark.

Next thing it shadows moonslicked laurels
or skims the lapped net on a tennis court.
Next thing it's ahead of you in the road.

What are you after? You keep swerving off,
flying blind over ashpits and netting wire;
invited by the brush of a word like *peignoir*,

rustles and glimpses, shot silk, the stealth of floods
So close to me I could hear her breathing
and there by the lighted window behind trees

it hangs in creepers matting the brickwork
and now it's a wet leaf blowing in the drive,
now soft-deckled, shadow-convolvulus

by the White Gates. Who would have thought it? At the
      White Gates
She let them do whatever they liked. Cling there
as long as you want. There is nothing to hide.

A Hazel Stick for Catherine Ann

The living mother-of-pearl of a salmon
just out of the water

is gone just like that, but your stick
is kept salmon-silver.

Seasoned and bendy,
it convinces the hand

that what you have you hold
to play with and pose with

and lay about with.
But then too it points back to cattle

and spatter and beating
the bars of a gate—

the very stick we might cut
from your family tree.

The living cobalt of an afternoon
dragonfly drew my eye to it first

and the evening I trimmed it for you
you saw your first glow-worm—

all of us stood round in silence, even you
gigantic enough to darken the sky

for a glow-worm.
And when I poked open the grass

a tiny brightening den lit the eye
in the blunt pared end of your stick.

A Kite for Michael and Christopher

All through that Sunday afternoon
a kite flew above Sunday,
a tightened drumhead, a flitter of blown chaff.

I'd seen it grey and slippy in the making,
I'd tapped it when it dried out white and stiff,
I'd tied the bows of newspaper
along its six-foot tail.

But now it was far up like a small black lark
and now it dragged as if the bellied string
were a wet rope hauled upon
to lift a shoal.

My friend says that the human soul
is about the weight of a snipe,
yet the soul at anchor there,
the string that sags and ascends,
weighs like a furrow assumed into the heavens.

Before the kite plunges down into the wood
and this line goes useless
take in your two hands, boys, and feel
the strumming, rooted, long-tailed pull of grief.
You were born fit for it.
Stand in here in front of me
and take the strain.

The Railway Children

When we climbed the slopes of the cutting
We were eye-level with the white cups
Of the telegraph poles and the sizzling wires.

Like lovely freehand they curved for miles
East and miles west beyond us, sagging
Under their burden of swallows.

We were small and thought we knew nothing
Worth knowing. We thought words travelled the wires
In the shiny pouches of raindrops,

Each one seeded full with the light
Of the sky, the gleam of the lines, and ourselves
So infinitesimally scaled

We could stream through the eye of a needle.

Widgeon

for Paul Muldoon

It had been badly shot.
While he was plucking it
he found, he says, the voice box—

like a flute stop
in the broken windpipe—

and blew upon it
unexpectedly
his own small widgeon cries.

Sheelagh na Gig

at Kilpeck

I

We look up at her
hunkered into her angle
under the eaves.

She bears the whole stone burden
on the small of her back and shoulders
and pinioned elbows,

the astute mouth, the gripping fingers
saying push, push hard,
push harder.

As the hips go high
her big tadpole forehead
is rounded out in sunlight.

And here beside her are two birds,
a rabbit's head, a ram's,
a mouth devouring heads.

II

Her hands holding herself
are like hands in an old barn
holding a bag open.

I was outside looking in
at its lapped and supple mouth
running grain.

I looked up under the thatch
at the dark mouth and eye
of a bird's nest or a rat hole,

smelling the rose on the wall,
mildew, an earthen floor,
the warm depth of the eaves.

And then one night in the yard
I stood still under heavy rain
wearing the bag like a caul.

III

We look up to her,
her ring-fort eyes,
her little slippy shoulders,

her nose incised and flat,
and feel light-headed looking up.
She is twig-boned, saddle-sexed,

grown-up, grown ordinary,
seeming to say,
'Yes, look at me to your heart's content

but look at every other thing.'
And here is a leaper in a kilt,
two figures kissing,

a mouth with sprigs,
a running hart, two fishes,
a damaged beast with an instrument.

'Aye'

(from *The Loaning*)

Big voices in the womanless kitchen.
They never lit a lamp in the summertime
but took the twilight as it came
like solemn trees. They sat on in the dark
with their pipes red in their mouths, the talk come down
to *Aye* and *Aye* again and, when the dog shifted,
a curt *There boy!*
                    I closed my eyes
to make the light motes stream behind them
and my head went airy, my chair rode
high and low among branches and the wind
stirred up a rookery in the next long *Aye*.

The King of the Ditchbacks

for John Montague

I

As if a trespasser
unbolted a forgotten gate
and ripped the growth
tangling its lower bars—

just beyond the hedge
he has opened a dark morse
along the bank,
a crooked wounding

of silent, cobwebbed
grass. If I stop
he stops
like the moon.

He lives in his feet
and ears, weather-eyed,
all pad and listening,
a denless mover.

Under the bridge
his reflection shifts
sideways to the current,
mothy, alluring.

I am haunted
by his stealthy rustling,
the unexpected spoor,
the pollen settling.

I was sure I knew him. The time I'd spent obsessively in that upstairs room bringing myself close to him: each entranced hiatus as I chainsmoked and stared out the dormer into the grassy hillside I was laying myself open. He was depending on me as I hung out on the limb of a translated phrase like a youngster dared out on to an alder branch over the whirlpool. Small dreamself in the branches. Dream fears I inclined towards, interrogating:

  —Are you the one I ran upstairs to find drowned under running water in the bath?
  —The one the mowing machine severed like a hare in the stiff frieze of harvest?
  —Whose little bloody clothes we buried in the garden?
  —The one who lay awake in darkness a wall's breadth from the troubled hoofs?

After I had dared these invocations, I went back towards the gate to follow him. And my stealth was second nature to me, as if I were coming into my own. I remembered I had been vested for this calling.

III

When I was taken aside that day
I had the sense of election:

they dressed my head in a fishnet
and plaited leafy twigs through meshes

so my vision was a bird's
at the heart of a thicket

and I spoke as I moved
like a voice from a shaking bush.

King of the ditchbacks,
I went with them obediently

to the edge of a pigeon wood—
deciduous canopy, screened wain of evening

we lay beneath in silence.
No birds came, but I waited

among briars and stones, or whispered
or broke the watery gossamers

if I moved a muscle.
'Come back to us,' they said, 'in harvest,

when we hide in the stooked corn,
when the gundogs can hardly retrieve

what's brought down.' And I saw myself
rising to move in that dissimulation,

top-knotted, masked in sheaves, noting
the fall of birds: a rich young man

leaving everything he had
for a migrant solitude.

Station Island

I

A hurry of bell-notes
flew over morning hush
and water-blistered cornfields,
an escaped ringing
that stopped as quickly

as it started. *Sunday*,
the silence breathed
and could not settle back
for a man had appeared
at the side of the field

with a bow-saw, held
stiffly up like a lyre.
He moved and stopped to gaze
up into hazel bushes,
angled his saw in,

pulled back to gaze again
and move on to the next.
'I know you, Simon Sweeney,
for an old Sabbath-breaker
who has been dead for years.'

'Damn all you know,' he said,
his eye still on the hedge
and not turning his head.
'I was your mystery man
and am again this morning.

Through gaps in the bushes,
your First Communion face

would watch me cutting timber.
When cut or broken limbs
of trees went yellow, when

woodsmoke sharpened air
or ditches rustled
you sensed my trail there
as if it had been sprayed.
It left you half afraid.

When they bade you listen
in the bedroom dark
to wind and rain in the trees
and think of tinkers camped
under a heeled-up cart

you shut your eyes and saw
a wet axle and spokes
in moonlight, and me
streaming from the shower,
headed for your door.'

Sunlight broke in the hazels,
the quick bell-notes began
a second time. I turned
at another sound:
a crowd of shawled women

were wading the young corn,
their skirts brushing softly.
Their motion saddened morning.
It whispered to the silence,
'Pray for us, pray for us,'

it conjured through the air
until the field was full
of half-remembered faces,
a loosed congregation
that straggled past and on.

As I drew behind them
I was a fasted pilgrim,
light-headed, leaving home
to face into my station.
'Stay clear of all processions!'

Sweeney shouted at me,
but the murmur of the crowd
and their feet slushing through
the tender, bladed growth
had opened a drugged path

I was set upon.
I trailed those early-risers
fallen into step
before the smokes were up.
The quick bell rang again.

II

I was parked on a high road, listening
to peewits and wind blowing round the car
when something came to life in the driving mirror,

someone walking fast in an overcoat
and boots, bareheaded, big, determined
in his sure haste along the crown of the road

so that I felt myself the challenged one.
The car door slammed. I was suddenly out
face to face with an aggravated man

raving on about nights spent listening for
gun butts to come cracking on the door,
yeomen on the rampage, and his neighbour

among them, hammering home the shape of things.
'Round about here you overtook the women,'
I said, as the thing came clear. 'Your *Lough Derg Pilgrim*

haunts me every time I cross this mountain—
as if I am being followed, or following.
I'm on my road there now to do the station.'

'O holy Jesus Christ, does nothing change?'
His head jerked sharply side to side and up
like a diver's surfacing after a plunge,

then with a look that said, *Who is this cub
anyhow*, he took cognizance again
of where he was: the road, the mountain top,

and the air, softened by a shower of rain,
worked on his anger visibly until:
'It is a road you travel on your own.

I who learned to read in the reek of flax
and smelled hanged bodies rotting on their gibbets
and saw their looped slime gleaming from the sacks—

hard-mouthed Ribbonmen and Orange bigots
made me into the old fork-tongued turncoat
who mucked the byre of their politics.

If times were hard, I could be hard too.
I made the traitor in me sink the knife.
And maybe there's a lesson there for you,

whoever you are, wherever you come out of,
for though there's something natural in your smile
there's something in it strikes me as defensive.'

'The angry role was never my vocation,'
I said. 'I come from County Derry,
where the last marching bands of Ribbonmen

on Patrick's Day still played their "Hymn to Mary".
Obedient strains like theirs tuned me first
and not that harp of unforgiving iron

the Fenians strung. A lot of what you wrote
I heard and did: this Lough Derg station,
flax-pullings, dances, fair-days, crossroads chat

and the shaky local voice of education.
All that. And always, Orange drums.
And neighbours on the roads at night with guns.'

'I know, I know, I know, I know,' he said,
'but you have to try to make sense of what comes.
Remember everything and keep your head.'

'The alders in the hedge,' I said, 'mushrooms,
dark-clumped grass where cows or horses dunged,
the cluck when pith-lined chestnut shells split open

in your hand, the melt of shells corrupting,
old jam pots in a drain clogged up with mud—'
But now Carleton was interrupting:

'All this is like a trout kept in a spring
or maggots sown in wounds for desperate ointment—'
another life that cleans our element.

We are earthworms of the earth, and all that
has gone through us is what will be our trace.'
He turned on his heel when he was saying this

and headed up the road at the same hard pace.

III

I knelt. Hiatus. Habit's afterlife . . .
I was back among bead clicks and the murmurs
from inside confessionals, side altars
where candles died insinuating slight

intimate smells of wax at body heat.
There was an active, wind-stilled hush, as if

in a shell the listened-for ocean stopped
and a tide rested and sustained the roof.

A seaside trinket floated then and idled
in vision, like phosphorescent weed,
a toy grotto with seedling mussel shells
and cockles glued in patterns over it,

pearls condensed from a child invalid's breath
into a shimmering ark, my house of gold
that housed the snowdrop weather of her death
long ago. I would stow away in the hold

of our big oak sideboard and forage for it
laid past in its tissue paper for good.
It was like touching birds' eggs, robbing the nest
of the word *wreath*, as kept and dry and secret

as her name, which they hardly ever spoke
but was a white bird trapped inside me
beating scared wings when *Health of the Sick*
fluttered its *pray for us* in the litany.

A cold draught blew under the kneeling boards.
I thought of walking round
and round a space utterly empty,
utterly a source, like the idea of sound

or like the absence sensed in swamp-fed air
above a ring of walked-down grass and rushes
where we once found the bad carcass and scrags of hair
of our dog that had disappeared weeks before.

IV

Blurred swimmings as I faced the sun, my back
to the stone pillar and the iron cross,
ready to say the dream words *I renounce* . . .

Blurred oval prints of newly ordained faces,
'Father' pronounced with a fawning relish,
the sunlit tears of parents being blessed.

I saw a young priest, glossy as a blackbird,
as if he had stepped from his anointing
a moment ago: his purple stole and cord

or cincture loosely tied, his polished shoes
unexpectedly secular beneath
a pleated, lace-hemmed alb of linen cloth.

His name had lain undisturbed for years
like an old bicycle wheel in a ditch
ripped at last from under jungling briars,

wet and perished. My arms were open wide
but I could not say the words. 'The rain forest,' he said,
'you've never seen the like of it. I lasted

only a couple of years. Bare-breasted
women and rat-ribbed men. Everything wasted.
I rotted like a pear. I sweated Masses . . .'

His breath came short and shorter. 'In long houses
I raised the chalice above headdresses.
In hoc signo . . . On that abandoned

mission compound, my vocation
is a steam off the drenched creepers.'
I had broken off from my renunciation

while he was speaking, so as to clear the way
for other pilgrims queueing to get started.
'I'm older now than you when you went away,'

I ventured, feeling a strange reversal.
'I never could see you on the foreign missions.
I could only see you on a bicycle,

a clerical student home for the summer,
doomed to the decent thing. Visiting neighbours.
Drinking tea and praising home-made bread.

Something in them would be ratified
when they saw you at the door in your black suit,
arriving like some sort of holy mascot.

You gave too much relief, you raised a siege
the world had laid against their kitchen grottoes
hung with holy pictures and crucifixes.'

'And you,' he faltered, 'what are you doing here
but the same thing? What possessed you?
I at least was young and unaware

that what I thought was chosen was convention.
But all this you were clear of you walked into
over again. And the god has, as they say, withdrawn.

What are you doing, going through these motions?
Unless . . . Unless . . .' Again he was short of breath
and his whole fevered body yellowed and shook.

'Unless you are here taking the last look.'
Then where he stood was empty as the roads
we both grew up beside, where the sick man

had taken his last look one drizzly evening
when the tarmac steamed with the first breath of spring,
a knee-deep mist I waded silently

behind him, on his circuits, visiting.

V

An old man's hands, like soft paws rowing forward,
groped for and warded off the air ahead.
Barney Murphy shuffled on the concrete.

Master Murphy. I heard the weakened voice
bulling in sudden rage all over again
and fell in behind, my eyes fixed on his heels
like a man lifting swathes at a mower's heels.
His sockless feet were like the dried broad bean
that split its stitches in the display jar
high on a window in the old classroom,
white as shy faces in the classroom door.
'Master,' those elders whispered, 'I wonder, master . . .'
rustling envelopes, proffering them, withdrawing,
waiting for him to sign beside their mark,
and 'Master' I repeated to myself
so that he stopped but did not turn or move,
gone quiet in the shoulders, his small head
vigilant in the cold gusts off the lough.
I moved ahead and faced him, shook his hand.

Above the winged collar, his mottled face
went distant in a smile as the voice
readied itself and husked and scraped, 'Good man,
good man yourself,' then lapsed again
into the limbo and dry urn of the larynx.
The Adam's apple in its weathered sac
worked like the plunger of a pump in drought
but yielded nothing to help the helpless smile.
Morning field smells came past on the wind,
the sex-cut of sweetbriar after rain,
new meadow hay, birds' nests filled with leaves.

'You'd have thought that Anahorish School
was purgatory enough for any man,'
I said. 'You have done your station.'
Then a little trembling happened and his breath
rushed the air softly as scythes in his lost meadows.
'Birch trees have overgrown Leitrim Moss,
dairy herds are grazing where the school was
and the school garden's loose black mould is grass.'
He was gone with that and I was faced wrong way
into more pilgrims absorbed in this exercise.
As I stood among their whispers and bare feet

the mists of all the mornings I'd set out
for Latin classes with him, face to face,
refreshed me. *Mensa, mensa, mensam*
sang on the air like a busy sharping-stone.

'We'll go some day to my uncle's farm at Toome—'
Another master spoke. *'For what is the great
moving power and spring of verse? Feeling, and
in particular, love.* When I went last year
I drank three cups of water from the well.
It was very cold. It stung me in the ears.
You should have met him—' Coming in as usual
with the rubbed quotation and his cocked bird's eye
dabbing for detail. *When you're on the road
give lifts to people, you'll always learn something.*
There he went, in his belted gaberdine,
and after him, another fosterer,
slack-shouldered and clear-eyed: 'Sure I might have known
once I had made the pad, you'd be after me
sooner or later. Forty-two years on
and you've got no farther! But after that again,
where else would you go? Iceland, maybe? Maybe the
        Dordogne?'

And then the parting shot. 'In my own day
the odd one came here on the hunt for women.'

        VI

Freckle-face, fox-head, pod of the broom,
Catkin-pixie, little fern-swish:
Where did she arrive from?
Like a wish wished
And gone, her I chose at 'secrets'
And whispered to. When we were playing houses.
I was sunstruck at the basilica door—
A stillness far away, a space, a dish,
A blackened tin and knocked-over stool—
Like a tramped neolithic floor
Uncovered among dunes where the bent grass

Whispers on like reeds about Midas's
Secrets, secrets. I shut my ears to the bell.
Head hugged. Eyes shut. Leaf ears. *Don't tell. Don't tell.*

A stream of pilgrims answering the bell
Trailed up the steps as I went down them
Towards the bottle-green, still
Shade of an oak. Shades of the Sabine farm
On the stone beds of St Patrick's Purgatory.
Late summer, country distance, not an air:
Loosen the toga for wine and poetry
Till Phoebus returning routs the morning star.
As a somnolent hymn to Mary rose
I felt an old pang that packed bags of grain
And the sloped shafts of forks and hoes
Once mocked me with, at my own long virgin
Fasts and thirsts, my nightly shadow feasts,
Haunting the granaries of words like *breasts.*

As if I knelt for years at a keyhole
Mad for it, and all that ever opened
Was the breathed-on grille of a confessional
Until that night I saw her honey-skinned
Shoulderblades and the wheatlands of her back
Through the wide keyhole of her keyhole dress
And a window facing the deep south of luck
Opened and I inhaled the land of kindness.
As little flowers that were all bowed and shut
By the night chills rise on their stems and open
As soon as they have felt the touch of sunlight,
So I revived in my own wilting powers
And my heart flushed, like somebody set free.
Translated, given, under the oak tree.

VII

I had come to the edge of the water,
soothed by just looking, idling over it
as if it were a clear barometer

or a mirror, when his reflection
did not appear but I sensed a presence
entering into my concentration

on not being concentrated as he spoke
my name. And though I was reluctant
I turned to meet his face and the shock

is still in me at what I saw. His brow
was blown open above the eye and blood
had dried on his neck and cheek. 'Easy now,'

he said, 'it's only me. You've seen men as raw
after a football match . . . What time it was
when I was wakened up I still don't know

but I heard this knocking, knocking, and it
scared me, like the phone in the small hours,
so I had the sense not to put on the light

but looked out from behind the curtain.
I saw two customers on the doorstep
and an old Land-Rover with the doors open

parked on the street, so I let the curtain drop;
but they must have been waiting for it to move
for they shouted to come down into the shop.

She started to cry then and roll round the bed,
lamenting and lamenting to herself,
not even asking who it was. "Is your head

astray, or what's come over you?" I roared, more
to bring myself to my senses
than out of any real anger at her

for the knocking shook me, the way they kept it up,
and her whingeing and half-screeching made it worse.
All the time they were shouting, "Shop!

Shop!" so I pulled on my shoes and a sportscoat
and went back to the window and called out,
"What do you want? Could you quieten the racket

or I'll not come down at all." "There's a child not well.
Open up and see what you have got—pills
or a powder or something in a bottle,"

one of them said. He stepped back off the footpath
so I could see his face in the streetlamp
and when the other moved I knew them both.

But bad and all as the knocking was, the quiet
hit me worse. She was quiet herself now,
lying dead still, whispering to watch out.

At the bedroom door I switched on the light.
"It's odd they didn't look for a chemist.
Who are they anyway at this hour of the night?"

she asked me, with the eyes standing in her head.
"I know them to see," I said, but something
made me reach and squeeze her hand across the bed

before I went downstairs into the aisle
of the shop. I stood there, going weak
in the legs. I remember the stale smell

of cooked meat or something coming through
as I went to open up. From then on
you know as much about it as I do.'

'Did they say nothing?' 'Nothing. What would they say?'
'Were they in uniform? Not masked in any way?'
'They were barefaced as they would be in the day,

shites thinking they were the be-all and the end-all.'
'Not that it is any consolation
but they were caught,' I told him, 'and got jail.'

Big-limbed, decent, open-faced, he stood
forgetful of everything now except
whatever was welling up in his spoiled head,

beginning to smile. 'You've put on a bit of weight
since you did your courting in that big Austin
you got the loan of on a Sunday night.'

Through life and death he had hardly aged.
There always was an athlete's cleanliness
shining off him, and except for the ravaged

forehead and the blood, he was still that same
rangy midfielder in a blue jersey
and starched pants, the one stylist on the team,

the perfect, clean, unthinkable victim.
'Forgive the way I have lived indifferent—
forgive my timid circumspect involvement,'

I surprised myself by saying. 'Forgive
my eye,' he said, 'all that's above my head.'
And then a stun of pain seemed to go through him

and he trembled like a heatwave and faded.

VIII

Black water. White waves. Furrows snowcapped.
A magpie flew from the basilica
and staggered in the granite airy space
I was staring into, on my knees
at the hard mouth of St Brigid's Bed.
I came to and there at the bed's stone hub
was my archaeologist, very like himself,
with his scribe's face smiling its straight-lipped smile,
starting at the sight of me with the same old
pretence of amazement, so that the wing
of wood-kerne's hair fanned down over his brow.

And then as if a shower were blackening
already blackened stubble, the dark weather
of his unspoken pain came over him.
A pilgrim bent and whispering on his rounds
inside the bed passed between us slowly.

'Those dreamy stars that pulsed across the screen
beside you in the ward—your heartbeats, Tom, I mean—
scared me the way they stripped things naked.
My banter failed too early in that visit.
I could not take my eyes off the machine.
I had to head back straightaway to Dublin,
guilty and empty, feeling I had said nothing
and that, as usual, I had somehow broken
covenants, and failed an obligation.
I half-knew we would never meet again . . .
Did our long gaze and last handshake contain
nothing to appease that recognition?'

'Nothing at all. But familiar stone
had me half-numbed to face the thing alone.
I loved my still-faced archaeology.
The small crab-apple physiognomies
on high crosses, carved heads in abbeys . . .
Why else dig in for years in that hard place
in a muck of bigotry under the walls
picking through shards and Williamite cannon balls?
But all that we just turned to banter too.
I felt that I should have seen far more of you
and maybe would have—but dead at thirty-two!
Ah poet, lucky poet, tell me why
what seemed deserved and promised passed me by?'

I could not speak. I saw a hoard of black
basalt axeheads, smooth as a beetle's back,
a cairn of stone force that might detonate,
the eggs of danger. And then I saw a face
he had once given me, a plaster cast
of an abbess, done by the Gowran master,
mild-mouthed and cowled, a character of grace.

'Your gift will be a candle in our house—'
But he had gone when I looked to meet his eyes
and hunkering instead there in his place
was a bleeding, pale-faced boy, plastered in mud.
'The red-hot pokers blazed a lovely red
in Jerpoint the Sunday I was murdered,'
he said quietly. 'Now do you remember?
You were there with poets when you got the word
and stayed there with them, while your own flesh and blood
was carted to Bellaghy from the Fews.
They showed more agitation at the news
than you did.'

       'But they were getting crisis
first-hand, Colum, they had happened in on
live sectarian assassination.
I was dumb, encountering what was destined.'
And so I pleaded with my second cousin.
'I kept seeing a grey stretch of Lough Beg
and the strand empty at daybreak.
I felt like the bottom of a dried-up lake.'

'You saw that, and you wrote that—not the fact.
You confused evasion and artistic tact.
The Protestant who shot me through the head
I accuse directly, but indirectly, you
who now atone perhaps upon this bed
for the way you whitewashed ugliness and drew
the lovely blinds of the *Purgatorio*
and saccharined my death with morning dew.'

Then I seemed to waken out of sleep
among more pilgrims whom I did not know
drifting to the hostel for the night.

IX

'My brain dried like spread turf, my stomach
Shrank to a cinder and tightened and cracked.
Often I was dogs on my own track

Of blood on wet grass that I could have licked.
Under the prison blanket, an ambush
Stillness I felt safe in settled round me.
Street lights came on in small towns, the bomb flash
Came before the sound, I saw country
I knew from Glenshane down to Toome
And heard a car I could make out years away
With me in the back of it like a white-faced groom,
A hit-man on the brink, emptied and deadly.
When the police yielded my coffin, I was light
As my head when I took aim.'
                              This voice from blight
And hunger died through the black dorm:
There he was, laid out with a drift of Mass cards
At his shrouded feet. Then the firing party's
Volley in the yard. I saw woodworm
In gate posts and door jambs, smelt mildew
From the byre loft where he had watched and hid
From fields that his draped coffin would raft through.
Unquiet soul, they should have buried you
In the bog where you threw your first grenade,
Where only helicopters and curlews
Make their maimed music, and sphagnum moss
Could teach you its medicinal repose
Until, when the weasel whistles on its tail,
No other weasel will obey its call.

I dreamt and drifted. All seemed to run to waste
As down a swirl of mucky, glittering flood
Strange polyp floated like a huge corrupt
Magnolia bloom, surreal as a shed breast,
My softly awash and blanching self-disgust.
And I cried among night waters, 'I repent
My unweaned life that kept me competent
To sleepwalk with connivance and mistrust.'
Then, like a pistil growing from the polyp,
A lighted candle rose and steadied up
Until the whole bright-masted thing retrieved
A course and the currents it had gone with

Were what it rode and showed. No more adrift,
My feet touched bottom and my heart revived.

Then something round and clear
And mildly turbulent, like a bubbleskin
Or a moon in smoothly rippled lough water
Rose in a cobwebbed space: the molten
Inside-sheen of an instrument
Revolved its polished convexes full
Upon me, so close and brilliant
I seemed to pitch back in a headlong fall.
And then it was the clarity of waking
To sunlight and a bell and gushing taps
In the next cubicle. Still there for the taking!
The old brass trumpet with its valves and stops
I found once in loft thatch, a mystery
I shied from then for I thought such trove beyond me.

'I hate how quick I was to know my place.
I hate where I was born, hate everything
That made me biddable and unforthcoming,'
I mouthed at my half-composed face
In the shaving mirror, like somebody
Drunk in the bathroom during a party,
Lulled and repelled by his own reflection.
As if the cairnstone could defy the cairn.
As if the eddy could reform the pool.
As if a stone swirled under a cascade,
Eroded and eroding in its bed,
Could grind itself down to a different core.
Then I thought of the tribe whose dances never fail
For they keep dancing till they sight the deer.

                X

Morning stir in the hostel. A pot
hooked on forged links. Soot flakes. Plumping water.
The open door brilliant with sunlight.
Hearthsmoke rambling and a thud of earthenware

drumming me back until I saw the mug
beyond my reach on its high shelf, the one
patterned with blue cornflowers, sprig after sprig
repeating round it, as quiet as a milestone . . .

When had it not been there? There was one night
when fit-up actors used it for a prop
and I sat in the dark hall estranged from it
as a couple vowed and called it their loving cup

and held it in our gaze until the curtain
jerked shut with an ordinary noise.
Dipped and glamoured then by this translation,
it was restored to its old haircracked doze

on the mantelpiece, its parchment glazes fast—
as the otter surfaced once with Ronan's psalter
miraculously unharmed, that had been lost
a day and a night under the lough water.

And so the saint praised God on the lough shore
for that dazzle of impossibility
I credited again in the sun-filled door,
so absolutely light it could put out fire.

XI

As if the prisms of the kaleidoscope
I plunged once in a butt of muddied water
surfaced like a marvellous lightship

and out of its silted crystals a monk's face
that had spoken years ago from behind a grille
spoke again about the need and chance

to salvage everything, to re-envisage
the zenith and glimpsed jewels of any gift
mistakenly abased . . .

What came to nothing could always be replenished.
'Read poems as prayers,' he said, 'and for your penance
translate me something by Juan de la Cruz.'

Returned from Spain to our chapped wilderness,
his consonants aspirate, his forehead shining,
he had made me feel there was nothing to confess.

Now his sandalled passage stirred me on to this:
How well I know that fountain, filling, running,
    although it is the night.

That eternal fountain, hidden away,
I know its haven and its secrecy
    although it is the night.

But not its source because it does not have one,
which is all sources' source and origin
    although it is the night.

No other thing can be so beautiful.
Here the earth and heaven drink their fill
    although it is the night.

So pellucid it never can be muddied,
and I know that all light radiates from it
    although it is the night.

I know no sounding-line can find its bottom,
nobody ford or plumb its deepest fathom
    although it is the night.

And its current so in flood it overspills
to water hell and heaven and all peoples
    although it is the night.

And the current that is generated there,
as far as it wills to, it can flow that far
    although it is the night.

And from these two a third current proceeds
which neither of these two, I know, precedes
    although it is the night.

This eternal fountain hides and splashes
within this living bread that is life to us
    although it is the night.

Hear it calling out to every creature.
And they drink these waters, although it is dark here
    because it is the night.

I am repining for this living fountain.
Within this bread of life I see it plain
    although it is the night.

XII

Like a convalescent, I took the hand
stretched down from the jetty, sensed again
an alien comfort as I stepped on ground

to find the helping hand still gripping mine,
fish-cold and bony, but whether to guide
or to be guided I could not be certain

for the tall man in step at my side
seemed blind, though he walked straight as a rush
upon his ashplant, his eyes fixed straight ahead.

Then I knew him in the flesh
out there on the tarmac among the cars,
wintered hard and sharp as a blackthorn bush.

His voice eddying with the vowels of all rivers
came back to me, though he did not speak yet,
a voice like a prosecutor's or a singer's,

cunning, narcotic, mimic, definite
as a steel nib's downstroke, quick and clean,
and suddenly he hit a litter basket

with his stick, saying, 'Your obligation
is not discharged by any common rite.
What you do you must do on your own.

The main thing is to write
for the joy of it. Cultivate a work-lust
that imagines its haven like your hands at night

dreaming the sun in the sunspot of a breast.
You are fasted now, light-headed, dangerous.
Take off from here. And don't be so earnest,

so ready for the sackcloth and the ashes.
Let go, let fly, forget.
You've listened long enough. Now strike your note.'

It was as if I had stepped free into space
alone with nothing that I had not known
already. Raindrops blew in my face

as I came to and heard the harangue and jeers
going on and on. 'The English language
belongs to us. You are raking at dead fires,

rehearsing the old whinges at your age.
That subject people stuff is a cod's game,
infantile, like this peasant pilgrimage.

You lose more of yourself than you redeem
doing the decent thing. Keep at a tangent.
When they make the circle wide, it's time to swim

out on your own and fill the element
with signatures on your own frequency,
echo-soundings, searches, probes, allurements,

elver-gleams in the dark of the whole sea.'
The shower broke in a cloudburst, the tarmac
fumed and sizzled. As he moved off quickly

the downpour loosed its screens round his straight walk.

from *Sweeney Redivivus*

The First Gloss

Take hold of the shaft of the pen.
Subscribe to the first step taken
from a justified line
into the margin.

Sweeney Redivivus

I stirred wet sand and gathered myself
to climb the steep-flanked mound,
my head like a ball of wet twine
dense with soakage, but beginning
to unwind.
                    Another smell
was blowing off the river, bitter
as night airs in a scutch mill.
The old trees were nowhere,
the hedges thin as penwork
and the whole enclosure lost
under hard paths and sharp-ridged houses.

And there I was, incredible to myself,
among people far too eager to believe me
and my story, even if it happened to be true.

In the Beech

I was a lookout posted and forgotten.

On one side under me, the concrete road.
On the other, the bullocks' covert,
the breath and plaster of a drinking place
where the school-leaver discovered peace
to touch himself in the reek of churned-up mud.

And the tree itself a strangeness and a comfort,
as much a column as a bole. The very ivy
puzzled its milk-tooth frills and tapers
over the grain: was it bark or masonry?

I watched the red-brick chimney rear
its stamen, course by course,
and the steeplejacks up there at their antics
like flies against the mountain.

I felt the tanks' advance beginning
at the cynosure of the growth rings,
then winced at their imperium refreshed
in each powdered bolt-mark on the concrete.
And the pilot with his goggles back came in
so low I could see the cockpit rivets.

My hidebound boundary tree. My tree of knowledge.
My thick-tapped, soft-fledged, airy listening post.

The First Kingdom

The royal roads were cow paths.
The queen mother hunkered on a stool
and played the harpstrings of milk
into a wooden pail.
With seasoned sticks the nobles
lorded it over the hindquarters of cattle.

Units of measurement were pondered
by the cartful, barrowful and bucketful.
Time was a backward rote of names and mishaps,
bad harvests, fires, unfair settlements,
deaths in floods, murders and miscarriages.

And if my rights to it all came only
by their acclamation, what was it worth?
I blew hot and blew cold.
They were two-faced and accommodating.
And seed, breed and generation still
they are holding on, every bit
as pious and exacting and demeaned.

The First Flight

It was more sleepwalk than spasm
yet that was a time when the times
were also in spasm—

the ties and the knots running through us
split open
down the lines of the grain.

As I drew close to pebbles and berries,
the smell of wild garlic, relearning
the acoustic of frost

and the meaning of woodnote,
my shadow over the field
was only a spin-off,

my empty place an excuse
for shifts in the camp, old rehearsals
of debts and betrayal.

Singly they came to the tree
with a stone in each pocket
to whistle and bill me back in

and I would collide and cascade
through leaves when they'd left,
my point of repose knocked askew.

I was mired in attachment
until they began to pronounce me
a feeder off battlefields

so I mastered new rungs of the air
to survey out of reach
their bonfires on hills, their hosting

and fasting, the levies from Scotland
as always, and the people of art
diverting their rhythmical chants

to fend off the onslaught of winds
I would welcome and climb
at the top of my bent.

Drifting Off

The guttersnipe and the albatross
gliding for days without a single wingbeat
were equally beyond me.

I yearned for the gannet's strike,
the unbegrudging concentration
of the heron.

In the camaraderie of rookeries,
in the spiteful vigilance of colonies
I was at home.

I learned to distrust
the allure of the cuckoo
and the gossip of starlings,

kept faith with doughty bullfinches,
levelled my wit too often
to the small-minded wren

and too often caved in
to the pathos of waterhens
and panicky corncrakes.

I gave much credence to stragglers,
overrated the composure of blackbirds
and the folklore of magpies.

But when goldfinch or kingfisher rent
the veil of the usual,
pinions whispered and braced

as I stooped, unwieldy
and brimming,
my spurs at the ready.

The Cleric

I heard new words prayed at cows
in the byre, found his sign
on the crock and the hidden still,

smelled fumes from his censer
in the first smokes of morning.
Next thing he was making a progress

through gaps, stepping out sites,
sinking his crozier deep
in the fort-hearth.

If he had stuck to his own
cramp-jawed abbesses and intoners
dibbling round the enclosure,

his Latin and blather of love,
his parchments and scheming
in letters shipped over water—

but no, he overbore
with his unctions and orders,
he had to get in on the ground.

History that planted its standards
on his gables and spires
ousted me to the marches

of skulking and whingeing.
Or did I desert?
Give him his due, in the end

he opened my path to a kingdom
of such scope and neuter allegiance
my emptiness reigns at its whim.

The Hermit

As he prowled the rim of his clearing
where the blade of choice had not spared
one stump of affection

he was like a ploughshare
interred to sustain the whole field
of force, from the bitted

and high-drawn sideways curve
of the horse's neck to the aim
held fast in the wrists and elbows—

the more brutal the pull
and the drive, the deeper
and quieter the work of refreshment.

The Master

He dwelt in himself
like a rook in an unroofed tower.

To get close I had to maintain
a climb up deserted ramparts
and not flinch, not raise an eye
to search for an eye on the watch
from his coign of seclusion.

Deliberately he would unclasp
his book of withholding
a page at a time, and it was nothing
arcane, just the old rules
we all had inscribed on our slates.
Each character blocked on the parchment secure
in its volume and measure.
Each maxim given its space.

Tell the truth. Do not be afraid.
Durable, obstinate notions,
like quarrymen's hammers and wedges
proofed by intransigent service.
Like coping stones where you rest
in the balm of the wellspring.

How flimsy I felt climbing down
the unrailed stairs on the wall,
hearing the purpose and venture
in a wingflap above me.

The Scribes

I never warmed to them.
If they were excellent they were petulant
and jaggy as the holly tree
they rendered down for ink.
And if I never belonged among them,
they could never deny me my place.

In the hush of the scriptorium
a black pearl kept gathering in them
like the old dry glut inside their quills.
In the margin of texts of praise
they scratched and clawed.
They snarled if the day was dark
or too much chalk had made the vellum bland
or too little left it oily.

Under the rumps of lettering
they herded myopic angers.
Resentment seeded in the uncurling
fernheads of their capitals.

Now and again I started up
miles away and saw in my absence
the sloped cursive of each back and felt them
perfect themselves against me page by page.

Let them remember this not inconsiderable
contribution to their jealous art.

Holly

It rained when it should have snowed.
When we went to gather holly

the ditches were swimming, we were wet
to the knees, our hands were all jags

and water ran up our sleeves.
There should have been berries

but the sprigs we brought into the house
gleamed like smashed bottle-glass.

Now here I am, in a room that is decked
with the red-berried, waxy-leafed stuff,

and I almost forget what it's like
to be wet to the skin or longing for snow.

I reach for a book like a doubter
and want it to flare round my hand,

a black-letter bush, a glittering shield-wall
cutting as holly and ice.

An Artist

I love the thought of his anger.
His obstinacy against the rock, his coercion
of the substance from green apples.

The way he was a dog barking
at the image of himself barking.
And his hatred of his own embrace
of working as the only thing that worked—
the vulgarity of expecting ever
gratitude or admiration, which
would mean a stealing from him.

The way his fortitude held and hardened
because he did what he knew.
His forehead like a hurled *boule*
travelling unpainted space
behind the apple and behind the mountain.

The Old Icons

Why, when it was all over, did I hold on to them?

A patriot with folded arms in a shaft of light:
the barred cell window and his sentenced face
are the only bright spots in the little etching.

An oleograph of snowy hills, the outlawed priest's
red vestments, with the redcoats toiling closer
and the lookout coming like a fox across the gaps.

And the old committee of the sedition-mongers,
so well turned out in their clasped brogues and waistcoats,
the legend of their names an informer's list

prepared by neat-cuffs, third from left, at rear,
more compelling than the rest of them,
pivoting an action that was his rack

and others' ruin, the very rhythm of his name
a register of dear-bought treacheries
grown transparent now, and inestimable.

In Illo Tempore

The big missal splayed
and dangled silky ribbons
of emerald and purple and watery white.

Intransitively we would assist,
confess, receive. The verbs
assumed us. We adored.

And we lifted our eyes to the nouns.
Altar-stone was dawn and monstrance noon,
the word 'rubric' itself a bloodshot sunset.

Now I live by a famous strand
where seabirds cry in the small hours
like incredible souls

and even the range wall of the promenade
that I press down on for conviction
hardly tempts me to credit it.

On the Road

The road ahead
kept reeling in
at a steady speed,
the verges dripped.

In my hands
like a wrested trophy,
the empty round
of the steering wheel.

The trance of driving
made all roads one:
the seraph-haunted, Tuscan
footpath, the green

oak-alleys of Dordogne
or that track through corn
where the rich young man
asked his question—

*Master, what must I
do to be saved?*
Or the road where the bird
with an earth-red back

and a white and black
tail, like parquet
of flint and jet,
wheeled over me

in visitation.
*Sell all you have
and give to the poor.*
I was up and away

like a human soul
that plumes from the mouth
in undulant, tenor
black-letter Latin.

I was one for sorrow,
Noah's dove,
a panicked shadow
crossing the deer path.

If I came to earth
it would be by way of
a small east window
I once squeezed through,

scaling heaven
by superstition,
drunk and happy
on a chapel gable.

I would roost a night
on the slab of exile,
then hide in the cleft
of that churchyard wall

where hand after hand
keeps wearing away
at the cold, hard-breasted
votive granite.

And follow me.
I would migrate
through a high cave mouth
into an oaten, sun-warmed cliff,

on down the soft-nubbed,
clay-floored passage,
face-brush, wingflap,
to the deepest chamber.

There a drinking deer
is cut into rock,
its haunch and neck
rise with the contours,

the incised outline
curves to a strained
expectant muzzle
and a nostril flared

at a dried-up source.
For my book of changes
I would meditate
that stone-faced vigil

until the long dumbfounded
spirit broke cover
to raise a dust
in the font of exhaustion.

Villanelle for an Anniversary

A spirit moved, John Harvard walked the yard,
The atom lay unsplit, the west unwon,
The books stood open and the gates unbarred.

The maps dreamt on like moondust. Nothing stirred.
The future was a verb in hibernation.
A spirit moved, John Harvard walked the yard.

Before the classic style, before the clapboard,
All through the small hours of an origin,
The books stood open and the gates unbarred.

Night passage of a migratory bird.
Wingflap. Gownflap. Like a homing pigeon
A spirit moved, John Harvard walked the yard.

Was that his soul (look) sped to its reward
By grace or works? A shooting star? An omen?
The books stood open and the gates unbarred.

Begin again where frosts and tests were hard.
Find yourself or founder. Here, imagine
A spirit moves, John Harvard walks the yard,
The books stand open and the gates unbarred.

FROM

The Haw Lantern

[1 9 8 7]

FOR BERNARD AND JANE McCABE

The riverbed, dried-up, half-full of leaves.

Us, listening to a river in the trees.

Alphabets

I

A shadow his father makes with joined hands
And thumbs and fingers nibbles on the wall
Like a rabbit's head. He understands
He will understand more when he goes to school.

There he draws smoke with chalk the whole first week,
Then draws the forked stick that they call a Y.
This is writing. A swan's neck and swan's back
Make the 2 he can see now as well as say.

Two rafters and a cross-tie on the slate
Are the letter some call *ah*, some call *ay*.
There are charts, there are headlines, there is a right
Way to hold the pen and a wrong way.

First it is 'copying out', and then 'English',
Marked correct with a little leaning hoe.
Smells of inkwells rise in the classroom hush.
A globe in the window tilts like a coloured O.

II

Declensions sang on air like a *hosanna*
As, column after stratified column,
Book One of *Elementa Latina*,
Marbled and minatory, rose up in him.

For he was fostered next in a stricter school
Named for the patron saint of the oak wood
Where classes switched to the pealing of a bell
And he left the Latin forum for the shade

Of new calligraphy that felt like home.
The letters of this alphabet were trees.
The capitals were orchards in full bloom,
The lines of script like briars coiled in ditches.

Here in her snooded garment and bare feet,
All ringleted in assonance and woodnotes,
The poet's dream stole over him like sunlight
And passed into the tenebrous thickets.

He learns this other writing. He is the scribe
Who drove a team of quills on his white field.
Round his cell door the blackbirds dart and dab.
Then self-denial, fasting, the pure cold.

By rules that hardened the farther they reached north
He bends to his desk and begins again.
Christ's sickle has been in the undergrowth.
The script grows bare and Merovingian.

III

The globe has spun. He stands in a wooden O.
He alludes to Shakespeare. He alludes to Graves.
Time has bulldozed the school and school window.
Balers drop bales like printouts where stooked sheaves

Made lambdas on the stubble once at harvest
And the delta face of each potato pit
Was patted straight and moulded against frost.
All gone, with the omega that kept

Watch above each door, the good-luck horseshoe.
Yet shape-note language, absolute on air
As Constantine's sky-lettered IN HOC SIGNO
Can still command him; or the necromancer

Who would hang from the domed ceiling of his house
A figure of the world with colours in it

So that the figure of the universe
And 'not just single things' would meet his sight

When he walked abroad. As from his small window
The astronaut sees all that he has sprung from,
The risen, aqueous, singular, lucent O
Like a magnified and buoyant ovum—

Or like my own wide pre-reflective stare
All agog at the plasterer on his ladder
Skimming our gable and writing our name there
With his trowel point, letter by strange letter.

Terminus

I

When I hoked there, I would find
An acorn and a rusted bolt.

If I lifted my eyes, a factory chimney
And a dormant mountain.

If I listened, an engine shunting
And a trotting horse.

Is it any wonder when I thought
I would have second thoughts?

II

When they spoke of the prudent squirrel's hoard
It shone like gifts at a Nativity.

When they spoke of the mammon of iniquity
The coins in my pockets reddened like stove-lids.

I was the march drain and the march drain's banks
Suffering the limit of each claim.

III

Two buckets were easier carried than one.
I grew up in between.

My left hand placed the standard iron weight.
My right tilted a last grain in the balance.

Baronies, parishes met where I was born.
When I stood on the central stepping stone

I was the last earl on horseback in midstream
Still parleying, in earshot of his peers.

From the Frontier of Writing

The tightness and the nilness round that space
when the car stops in the road, the troops inspect
its make and number and, as one bends his face

towards your window, you catch sight of more
on a hill beyond, eyeing with intent
down cradled guns that hold you under cover,

and everything is pure interrogation
until a rifle motions and you move
with guarded unconcerned acceleration—

a little emptier, a little spent
as always by that quiver in the self,
subjugated, yes, and obedient.

So you drive on to the frontier of writing
where it happens again. The guns on tripods;
the sergeant with his on-off mike repeating

data about you, waiting for the squawk
of clearance; the marksman training down
out of the sun upon you like a hawk.

And suddenly you're through, arraigned yet freed,
as if you'd passed from behind a waterfall
on the black current of a tarmac road

past armour-plated vehicles, out between
the posted soldiers flowing and receding
like tree shadows into the polished windscreen.

The Haw Lantern

The wintry haw is burning out of season,
crab of the thorn, a small light for small people,
wanting no more from them but that they keep
the wick of self-respect from dying out,
not having to blind them with illumination.

But sometimes when your breath plumes in the frost
it takes the roaming shape of Diogenes
with his lantern, seeking one just man;
so you end up scrutinized from behind the haw
he holds up at eye-level on its twig,
and you flinch before its bonded pith and stone,
its blood-prick that you wish would test and clear you,
its pecked-at ripeness that scans you, then moves on.

From the Republic of Conscience

I

When I landed in the republic of conscience
it was so noiseless when the engines stopped
I could hear a curlew high above the runway.

At immigration, the clerk was an old man
who produced a wallet from his homespun coat
and showed me a photograph of my grandfather.

The woman in customs asked me to declare
the words of our traditional cures and charms
to heal dumbness and avert the evil eye.

No porters. No interpreter. No taxi.
You carried your own burden and very soon
your symptoms of creeping privilege disappeared.

II

Fog is a dreaded omen there but lightning
spells universal good and parents hang
swaddled infants in trees during thunderstorms.

Salt is their precious mineral. And seashells
are held to the ear during births and funerals.
The base of all inks and pigments is seawater.

Their sacred symbol is a stylized boat.
The sail is an ear, the mast a sloping pen,
the hull a mouth-shape, the keel an open eye.

At their inauguration, public leaders
must swear to uphold unwritten law and weep
to atone for their presumption to hold office—

and to affirm their faith that all life sprang
from salt in tears which the sky-god wept
after he dreamt his solitude was endless.

III

I came back from that frugal republic
with my two arms the one length, the customs woman
having insisted my allowance was myself.

The old man rose and gazed into my face
and said that was official recognition
that I was now a dual citizen.

He therefore desired me when I got home
to consider myself a representative
and to speak on their behalf in my own tongue.

Their embassies, he said, were everywhere
but operated independently
and no ambassador would ever be relieved.

Hailstones

I

My cheek was hit and hit:
sudden hailstones
pelted and bounced on the road.

When it cleared again
something whipped and knowledgeable
had withdrawn

and left me there with my chances.
I made a small hard ball
of burning water running from my hand

just as I make this now
out of the melt of the real thing
smarting into its absence.

II

To be reckoned with, all the same,
those brats of showers.
The way they refused permission,

rattling the classroom window
like a ruler across the knuckles,
the way they were perfect first

and then in no time dirty slush.
Thomas Traherne had his orient wheat
for proof and wonder

but for us, it was the sting of hailstones
and the unstingable hands of Eddie Diamond
foraging in the nettles.

III

Nipple and hive, bite-lumps,
small acorns of the almost pleasurable
intimated and disallowed

when the shower ended
and everything said *wait.*
For what? For forty years

to say there, there you had
the truest foretaste of your aftermath—
in that dilation

when the light opened in silence
and a car with wipers going still
laid perfect tracks in the slush.

The Stone Verdict

When he stands in the judgement place
With his stick in his hand and the broad hat
Still on his head, maimed by self-doubt
And an old disdain of sweet talk and excuses,
It will be no justice if the sentence is blabbed out.
He will expect more than words in the ultimate court
He relied on through a lifetime's speechlessness.

Let it be like the judgement of Hermes,
God of the stone heap, where the stones were verdicts
Cast solidly at his feet, piling up around him
Until he stood waist-deep in the cairn
Of his own absolution: maybe a gate-pillar
Or a tumbled wallstead where hogweed earths the silence
Somebody will break at last to say, 'Here
His spirit lingers,' and will have said too much.

The Spoonbait

So a new similitude is given us
And we say: The soul may be compared

Unto a spoonbait that a child discovers
Beneath the sliding lid of a pencil case,

Glimpsed once and imagined for a lifetime
Risen and free and spooling out of nowhere—

A shooting star going back up the darkness.
It flees him and it burns him all at once

Like the single drop that Dives implored
Falling and falling into a great gulf.

Then exit, the polished helmet of a hero
Laid out amidships above scudding water.

Exit, alternatively, a toy of light
Reeled through him upstream, snagging on nothing.

Clearances

in memoriam M.K.H., 1911–1984

She taught me what her uncle once taught her:
How easily the biggest coal block split
If you got the grain and hammer angled right.

The sound of that relaxed alluring blow,
Its co-opted and obliterated echo,
Taught me to hit, taught me to loosen,

Taught me between the hammer and the block
To face the music. Teach me now to listen,
To strike it rich behind the linear black.

I

A cobble thrown a hundred years ago
Keeps coming at me, the first stone
Aimed at a great-grandmother's turncoat brow.
The pony jerks and the riot's on.
She's crouched low in the trap
Running the gauntlet that first Sunday
Down the brae to Mass at a panicked gallop.
He whips on through the town to cries of 'Lundy!'

Call her 'The Convert'. 'The Exogamous Bride'.
Anyhow, it is a genre piece
Inherited on my mother's side
And mine to dispose with now she's gone.
Instead of silver and Victorian lace,
The exonerating, exonerated stone.

II

Polished linoleum shone there. Brass taps shone.
The china cups were very white and big—
An unchipped set with sugar bowl and jug.
The kettle whistled. Sandwich and tea scone
Were present and correct. In case it run,
The butter must be kept out of the sun.
And don't be dropping crumbs. Don't tilt your chair.
Don't reach. Don't point. Don't make noise when you stir.

It is Number 5, New Row, Land of the Dead,
Where grandfather is rising from his place
With spectacles pushed back on a clean bald head
To welcome a bewildered homing daughter
Before she even knocks. 'What's this? What's this?'
And they sit down in the shining room together.

III

When all the others were away at Mass
I was all hers as we peeled potatoes.
They broke the silence, let fall one by one
Like solder weeping off the soldering iron:
Cold comforts set between us, things to share
Gleaming in a bucket of clean water.
And again let fall. Little pleasant splashes
From each other's work would bring us to our senses.

So while the parish priest at her bedside
Went hammer and tongs at the prayers for the dying
And some were responding and some crying
I remembered her head bent towards my head,
Her breath in mine, our fluent dipping knives—
Never closer the whole rest of our lives.

IV

Fear of affectation made her affect
Inadequacy whenever it came to
Pronouncing words 'beyond her'. *Bertold Brek.*
She'd manage something hampered and askew
Every time, as if she might betray
The hampered and inadequate by too
Well-adjusted a vocabulary.
With more challenge than pride, she'd tell me, 'You
Know all them things.' So I governed my tongue
In front of her, a genuinely well-
Adjusted adequate betrayal
Of what I knew better. I'd *naw* and *aye*
And decently relapse into the wrong
Grammar which kept us allied and at bay.

V

The cool that came off sheets just off the line
Made me think the damp must still be in them
But when I took my corners of the linen
And pulled against her, first straight down the hem
And then diagonally, then flapped and shook
The fabric like a sail in a cross-wind,
They made a dried-out undulating thwack.
So we'd stretch and fold and end up hand to hand
For a split second as if nothing had happened
For nothing had that had not always happened
Beforehand, day by day, just touch and go,
Coming close again by holding back
In moves where I was x and she was o
Inscribed in sheets she'd sewn from ripped-out flour sacks.

VI

In the first flush of the Easter holidays
The ceremonies during Holy Week
Were highpoints of our *Sons and Lovers* phase.
The midnight fire. The paschal candlestick.
Elbow to elbow, glad to be kneeling next
To each other up there near the front
Of the packed church, we would follow the text
And rubrics for the blessing of the font.
As the hind longs for the streams, so my soul . . .
Dippings. Towellings. The water breathed on.
The water mixed with chrism and with oil.
Cruet tinkle. Formal incensation
And the psalmist's outcry taken up with pride:
Day and night my tears have been my bread.

VII

In the last minutes he said more to her
Almost than in all their life together.
'You'll be in New Row on Monday night
And I'll come up for you and you'll be glad
When I walk in the door . . . Isn't that right?'
His head was bent down to her propped-up head.
She could not hear but we were overjoyed.
He called her good and girl. Then she was dead,
The searching for a pulsebeat was abandoned
And we all knew one thing by being there.
The space we stood around had been emptied
Into us to keep, it penetrated
Clearances that suddenly stood open.
High cries were felled and a pure change happened.

VIII

I thought of walking round and round a space
Utterly empty, utterly a source
Where the decked chestnut tree had lost its place
In our front hedge above the wallflowers.
The white chips jumped and jumped and skited high.
I heard the hatchet's differentiated
Accurate cut, the crack, the sigh
And collapse of what luxuriated
Through the shocked tips and wreckage of it all.
Deep-planted and long gone, my coeval
Chestnut from a jam jar in a hole,
Its heft and hush become a bright nowhere,
A soul ramifying and forever
Silent, beyond silence listened for.

The Milk Factory

Scuts of froth swirled from the discharge pipe.
We halted on the other bank and watched
A milky water run from the pierced side
Of milk itself, the crock of its substance spilt
Across white limbo floors where shift-workers
Waded round the clock, and the factory
Kept its distance like a bright-decked star-ship.

There we go, soft-eyed calves of the dew,
Astonished and assumed into fluorescence.

The Wishing Tree

I thought of her as the wishing tree that died
And saw it lifted, root and branch, to heaven,
Trailing a shower of all that had been driven

Need by need by need into its hale
Sap-wood and bark: coin and pin and nail
Came streaming from it like a comet-tail

New-minted and dissolved. I had a vision
Of an airy branch-head rising through damp cloud,
Of turned-up faces where the tree had stood.

Grotus and Coventina

Far from home Grotus dedicated an altar to Coventina
Who holds in her right hand a waterweed
And in her left a pitcher spilling out a river.
Anywhere Grotus looked at running water he felt at home
And when he remembered the stone where he cut his name
Some dried-up course beneath his breastbone started
Pouring and darkening—more or less the way
The thought of his stunted altar works on me.

Remember when our electric pump gave out,
Priming it with bucketfuls, our idiotic rage
And hangdog phone-calls to the farm next door
For somebody please to come and fix it?
And when it began to hammer on again,
Jubilation at the tap's full force, the sheer
Given fact of water, how you felt you'd never
Waste one drop but know its worth better always.
Do you think we could run through all that one more time?
I'll be Grotus, you be Coventina.

Wolfe Tone

Light as a skiff, manoeuvrable
yet outmanoeuvred,

I affected epaulettes and a cockade,
wrote a style well-bred and impervious

to the solidarity I angled for,
and played the ancient Roman with a razor.

I was the shouldered oar that ended up
far from the brine and whiff of venture,

like a scratching-post or a crossroads flagpole,
out of my element among small farmers—

I who once wakened to the shouts of men
rising from the bottom of the sea,

men in their shirts mounting through deep water
when the Atlantic stove our cabin's dead lights in

and the big fleet split and Ireland dwindled
as we ran before the gale under bare poles.

From the Canton of Expectation

I

We lived deep in a land of optative moods,
under high, banked clouds of resignation.
A rustle of loss in the phrase *Not in our lifetime*,
the broken nerve when we prayed *Vouchsafe* or *Deign*,
were creditable, sufficient to the day.

Once a year we gathered in a field
of dance platforms and tents where children sang
songs they had learned by rote in the old language.
An auctioneer who had fought in the brotherhood
enumerated the humiliations
we always took for granted, but not even he
considered this, I think, a call to action.
Iron-mouthed loudspeakers shook the air
yet nobody felt blamed. He had confirmed us.
When our rebel anthem played the meeting shut
we turned for home and the usual harassment
by militiamen on overtime at roadblocks.

II

And next thing, suddenly, this change of mood.
Books open in the newly wired kitchens.
Young heads that might have dozed a life away
against the flanks of milking cows were busy
paving and pencilling their first causeways
across the prescribed texts. The paving stones
of quadrangles came next and a grammar
of imperatives, the new age of demands.
They would banish the conditional for ever,
this generation born impervious to
the triumph in our cries of *de profundis*.

Our faith in winning by enduring most
they made anathema, intelligences
brightened and unmannerly as crowbars.

III

What looks the strongest has outlived its term.
The future lies with what's affirmed from under.
These things that corroborated us when we dwelt
under the aegis of our stealthy patron,
the guardian angel of passivity,
now sink a fang of menace in my shoulder.
I repeat the word 'stricken' to myself
and stand bareheaded under the banked clouds
edged more and more with brassy thunderlight.
I yearn for hammerblows on clinkered planks,
the uncompromised report of driven thole-pins,
to know there is one among us who never swerved
from all his instincts told him was right action,
who stood his ground in the indicative,
whose boat will lift when the cloudburst happens.

The Mud Vision

Statues with exposed hearts and barbed-wire crowns
Still stood in alcoves, hares flitted beneath
The dozing bellies of jets, our menu-writers
And punks with aerosol sprays held their own
With the best of them. Satellite link-ups
Wafted over us the blessings of popes, heliports
Maintained a charmed circle for idols on tour
And casualties on their stretchers. We sleepwalked
The line between panic and formulae, screentested
Our first native models and the last of the mummers,
Watching ourselves at a distance, advantaged
And airy as a man on a springboard
Who keeps limbering up because the man cannot dive.

And then in the foggy midlands it appeared,
Our mud vision, as if a rose window of mud
Had invented itself out of the glittery damp,
A gossamer wheel, concentric with its own hub
Of nebulous dirt, sullied yet lucent.
We had heard of the sun standing still and the sun
That changed colour, but we were vouchsafed
Original clay, transfigured and spinning.
And then the sunsets ran murky, the wiper
Could never entirely clean off the windscreen,
Reservoirs tasted of silt, a light fuzz
Accrued in the hair and the eyebrows, and some
Took to wearing a smudge on their foreheads
To be prepared for whatever. Vigils
Began to be kept around puddled gaps,
On altars bulrushes ousted the lilies
And a rota of invalids came and went
On beds they could lease placed in range of the shower.

A generation who had seen a sign!
Those nights when we stood in an umber dew and smelled

Mould in the verbena, or woke to a light
Furrow-breath on the pillow, when the talk
Was all about who had seen it and our fear
Was touched with a secret pride, only ourselves
Could be adequate then to our lives. When the rainbow
Curved flood-brown and ran like a water-rat's back
So that drivers on the hard shoulder switched off to watch,
We wished it away, and yet we presumed it a test
That would prove us beyond expectation.

We lived, of course, to learn the folly of that.
One day it was gone and the east gable
Where its trembling corolla had balanced
Was starkly a ruin again, with dandelions
Blowing high up on the ledges, and moss
That slumbered on through its increase. As cameras raked
The site from every angle, experts
Began their *post factum* jabber and all of us
Crowded in tight for the big explanations.
Just like that, we forgot that the vision was ours,
Our one chance to know the incomparable
And dive to a future. What might have been origin
We dissipated in news. The clarified place
Had retrieved neither us nor itself—except
You could say we survived. So say that, and watch us
Who had our chance to be mud-men, convinced and estranged,
Figure in our own eyes for the eyes of the world.

The Disappearing Island

Once we presumed to found ourselves for good
Between its blue hills and those sandless shores
Where we spent our desperate night in prayer and vigil,

Once we had gathered driftwood, made a hearth
And hung our cauldron in its firmament,
The island broke beneath us like a wave.

The land sustaining us seemed to hold firm
Only when we embraced it *in extremis*.
All I believe that happened there was vision.

The Riddle

You never saw it used but still can hear
The sift and fall of stuff hopped on the mesh,

Clods and buds in a little dust-up,
The dribbled pile accruing under it.

Which would be better, what sticks or what falls through?
Or does the choice itself create the value?

Legs apart, deft-handed, start a mime
To sift the sense of things from what's imagined

And work out what was happening in that story
Of the man who carried water in a riddle.

Was it culpable ignorance, or was it rather
A *via negativa* through drops and let-downs?

FROM

The Cure at Troy

[1 9 9 0]

Voices from Lemnos

I

CHORUS
Philoctetes.
       Hercules.
            Odysseus.
Heroes. Victims. Gods and human beings.
All throwing shapes, every one of them
Convinced he's in the right, all of them glad
To repeat themselves and their every last mistake,
No matter what.

             People so deep into
Their own self-pity self-pity buoys them up.
People so staunch and true, they are pillars of truth,
Shining with self-regard like polished stones.
And their whole life spent admiring themselves
For their own long-suffering.
                      Highlighting old scars
And flashing them around like decorations.
I hate it, I always hated it, I am
A part of it myself.

II

PHILOCTETES TO NEOPTOLEMUS
Gods curse it!
             But it's me the gods have cursed.
They've let my name and story be wiped out.
The real offenders got away with it
And I am still here, rotting like a leper.
Tell me, son. Achilles was your father.
Did you ever maybe hear him mentioning
A man who had inherited a bow—

The actual bow and arrows that belonged
To Hercules, and that Hercules gave him?
Did you never hear, son, about Philoctetes?
About the snake-bite he got at a shrine
When the first fleet was voyaging to Troy?
And then the way he broke out with a sore
And was marooned on the commanders' orders?
Let me tell you, son, the way they deserted me.
The sea and the sea-swell had me all worn out
So I dozed and fell asleep under a rock
Down on the shore.
                And there and then, like that,
They headed off.
             And they were delighted.
                And the only thing
They left me was a bundle of old rags.
Some day I want them all to waken up
The way I did that day. Imagine, son.
The bay all empty. The ships all disappeared.
Absolute loneliness. Nothing there except
The beat of the waves and the beat of my raw wound . . .

This island is a nowhere. Nobody
Would ever put in here. There's nothing.
Nothing to attract a lookout's eye.
Nobody in his right mind would come near it.
And the rare ones that ever did turn up
Landed by accident, against their will.
They would take pity on me, naturally.
Share out their supplies and give me clothes.
But not a one of them would ever, ever
Take me on board with them to ship me home.

     Every day has been a weeping wound
For ten years now. Ten years of misery—
That's all my service ever got for me.
That's what I've got to thank Odysseus for
And Menelaus and Agamemnon.
               Gods curse them all!
I ask for the retribution I deserve.

III

PHILOCTETES
Have you not a sword for me? Or an axe? Or something?

CHORUS
What for?

PHILOCTETES
            What for? What do you think for?
For foot and head and hand. For the relief
Of cutting myself off. I want away.

CHORUS
Away where?

PHILOCTETES
            Away to the house of death.
To my father, sitting waiting
Under the clay roof. I'll come back in to him
Out of the light, out of his memory
Of the day I left.
                    We'll be on the riverbank
Again, and see the Greeks arriving
And me setting out for Troy, in all good faith.

IV

CHORUS
Human beings suffer.
They torture one another.
They get hurt and get hard.
No poem or play or song
Can fully right a wrong
Inflicted and endured.

History says, Don't hope
On this side of the grave,
But then, once in a lifetime

The longed-for tidal wave
Of justice can rise up
And hope and history rhyme.

So hope for a great sea-change
On the far side of revenge.
Believe that a farther shore
Is reachable from here.
Believe in miracles
And cures and healing wells.

Call miracle self-healing,
The utter self-revealing
Double-take of feeling.
If there's fire on the mountain
And lightning and storm
And a god speaks from the sky

That means someone is hearing
The outcry and the birth-cry
Of new life at its term.
It means once in a lifetime
That justice can rise up
And hope and history rhyme.

PHILOCTETES
Hercules:
   I saw him in the fire.
Hercules
   was shining in the air.
I heard the voice of Hercules in my head.

CHORUS
I have opened the closed road
Between the living and the dead
To make the right road clear to you.
I am the voice of Hercules now.

Here on earth my labours were
The stepping stones to upper air.
Lives that suffer and come right
Are backlit by immortal light.

Go, Philoctetes, with this boy,
Go and be cured and capture Troy.
Asclepius will make you whole,
Relieve your body and your soul.

Go, with your bow. Conclude the sore
And cruel stalemate of our war.
Win by fair combat. But know to shun
Reprisal killings when that's done.

Then take just spoils and sail at last
Out of the bad dream of your past.
Make sacrifice. Burn spoils to me.
Shoot arrows in my memory.

But when the city's being sacked
Preserve the shrines. Show gods respect.
Reverence for gods survives
Our individual mortal lives.

V

CHORUS
Now it's high watermark
And floodtide in the heart
And time to go.
The sea-nymphs in the spray
Will be the chorus now.
What's left to say?

Suspect too much sweet talk
But never close your mind.

It was a fortunate wind
That blew me here. I leave
Half-ready to believe
That a crippled trust might walk

And the half-true rhyme is love.

FROM

Seeing Things

[1 9 9 1]

The Golden Bough

(*from* VIRGIL, *Aeneid*, Book VI)

Aeneas was praying and holding on the altar
When the prophetess started to speak: 'Blood relation of gods,
Trojan, son of Anchises, the way down to Avernus is easy.
Day and night black Pluto's door stands open.
But to retrace your steps and get back to upper air,
This is the real task and the real undertaking.
A few have been able to do it, sons of the gods
Favoured by Jupiter Justus, or exalted to heaven
In a blaze of heroic glory. Forests spread half-way down
And Cocytus winds through the dark, licking its banks.
Still, if love torments you so much and you so much desire
To sail the Stygian lake twice and twice to inspect
The underworld dark, if you must go beyond what's
        permitted,
Understand what you must do beforehand.
Hidden in the thick of a tree is a bough made of gold
And its leaves and pliable twigs are made of it too.
It is sacred to underworld Juno, who is its patron,
And overtopped by a grove where deep shadows mass
Along far wooded valleys. No one is ever permitted
To go down into earth's hidden places unless he has first
Plucked this golden-fledged tree-branch out of its tree
And bestowed it on fair Proserpina, to whom it belongs
By decree, her own special gift. And when it is plucked
A second one grows in its place, golden once more,
And the foliage growing upon it glimmers the same.
Therefore look up and search deep and when you have found
        it
Take hold of it boldly and duly. If fate has called you
The bough will come away easily, of its own sweet accord.
Otherwise, no matter how much strength you muster, you
        won't
Ever manage to quell it or fell it with the toughest of blades.'

Markings

I

We marked the pitch: four jackets for four goalposts,
That was all. The corners and the squares
Were there like longitude and latitude
Under the bumpy ground, to be
Agreed about or disagreed about
When the time came. And then we picked the teams
And crossed the line our called names drew between us.

Youngsters shouting their heads off in a field
As the light died and they kept on playing
Because by then they were playing in their heads
And the actual kicked ball came to them
Like a dream heaviness, and their own hard
Breathing in the dark and skids on grass
Sounded like effort in another world . . .
It was quick and constant, a game that never need
Be played out. Some limit had been passed,
There was fleetness, furtherance, untiredness
In time that was extra, unforeseen and free.

II

You also loved lines pegged out in the garden,
The spade nicking the first straight edge along
The tight white string. Or string stretched perfectly
To make the outline of a house foundation,
Pale timber battens set at right angles
For every corner, each freshly sawn new board
Spick and span in the oddly passive grass.
Or the imaginary line straight down
A field of grazing, to be ploughed open
From the rod stuck in one headrig to the rod
Stuck in the other.

III

All these things entered you
As if they were both the door and what came through it.
They marked the spot, marked time and held it open.
A mower parted the bronze sea of corn.
A windlass hauled the centre out of water.
Two men with a cross-cut kept it swimming
Into a felled beech backwards and forwards
So that they seemed to row the steady earth.

Man and Boy

'Catch the old one first,'
(My father's joke was also old, and heavy
And predictable). 'Then the young ones
Will all follow, and Bob's your uncle.'

On slow bright river evenings, the sweet time
Made him afraid we'd take too much for granted
And so our spirits must be lightly checked.

Blessed be down-to-earth! Blessed be highs!
Blessed be the detachment of dumb love
In that broad-backed, low-set man
Who feared debt all his life, but now and then
Could make a splash like the salmon he said was
'As big as a wee pork pig by the sound of it'.

II

In earshot of the pool where the salmon jumped
Back through its own unheard concentric soundwaves
A mower leans forever on his scythe.

He has mown himself to the centre of the field
And stands in a final perfect ring
Of sunlit stubble.

'Go and tell your father,' the mower says
(He said it to my father who told me),
'I have it mowed as clean as a new sixpence.'

My father is a barefoot boy with news,
Running at eye-level with weeds and stooks
On the afternoon of his own father's death.

The open, black half of the half-door waits.
I feel much heat and hurry in the air.
I feel his legs and quick heels far away

And strange as my own—when he will piggyback me
At a great height, light-headed and thin-boned,
Like a witless elder rescued from the fire.

Seeing Things

I

Inishbofin on a Sunday morning.
Sunlight, turfsmoke, seagulls, boatslip, diesel.
One by one we were being handed down
Into a boat that slipped and shilly-shallied
Scaresomely every time. We sat tight
On short cross-benches, in nervous twos and threes,
Obedient, newly close, nobody speaking
Except the boatmen, as the gunwales sank
And seemed they might ship water any minute.
The sea was very calm but even so,
When the engine kicked and our ferryman
Swayed for balance, reaching for the tiller,
I panicked at the shiftiness and heft
Of the craft itself. What guaranteed us—
That quick response and buoyancy and swim—
Kept me in agony. All the time
As we went sailing evenly across
The deep, still, seeable-down-into water,
It was as if I looked from another boat
Sailing through air, far up, and could see
How riskily we fared into the morning,
And loved in vain our bare, bowed, numbered heads.

II

Claritas. The dry-eyed Latin word
Is perfect for the carved stone of the water
Where Jesus stands up to his unwet knees
And John the Baptist pours out more water
Over his head: all this in bright sunlight
On the façade of a cathedral. Lines
Hard and thin and sinuous represent

The flowing river. Down between the lines
Little antic fish are all go. Nothing else.
And yet in that utter visibility
The stone's alive with what's invisible:
Waterweed, stirred sand-grains hurrying off,
The shadowy, unshadowed stream itself.
All afternoon, heat wavered on the steps
And the air we stood up to our eyes in wavered
Like the zig-zag hieroglyph for life itself.

III

Once upon a time my undrowned father
Walked into our yard. He had gone to spray
Potatoes in a field on the riverbank
And wouldn't bring me with him. The horse-sprayer
Was too big and new-fangled, bluestone might
Burn me in the eyes, the horse was fresh, I
Might scare the horse, and so on. I threw stones
At a bird on the shed roof, as much for
The clatter of the stones as anything,
But when he came back, I was inside the house
And saw him out the window, scatter-eyed
And daunted, strange without his hat,
His step unguided, his ghosthood immanent.
When he was turning on the riverbank,
The horse had rusted and reared up and pitched
Cart and sprayer and everything off balance
So the whole rig went over into a deep
Whirlpool, hoofs, chains, shafts, cartwheels, barrel
And tackle, all tumbling off the world,
And the hat already merrily swept along
The quieter reaches. That afternoon
I saw him face to face, he came to me
With his damp footprints out of the river,
And there was nothing between us there
That might not still be happily ever after.

An August Night

His hands were warm and small and knowledgeable.
When I saw them again last night, they were two ferrets,
Playing all by themselves in a moonlit field.

Field of Vision

I remember this woman who sat for years
In a wheelchair, looking straight ahead
Out the window at sycamore trees unleafing
And leafing at the far end of the lane.

Straight out past the TV in the corner,
The stunted, agitated hawthorn bush,
The same small calves with their backs to wind and rain,
The same acre of ragwort, the same mountain.

She was steadfast as the big window itself.
Her brow was clear as the chrome bits of the chair.
She never lamented once and she never
Carried a spare ounce of emotional weight.

Face to face with her was an education
Of the sort you got across a well-braced gate—
One of those lean, clean, iron, roadside ones
Between two whitewashed pillars, where you could see

Deeper into the country than you expected
And discovered that the field behind the hedge
Grew more distinctly strange as you kept standing
Focused and drawn in by what barred the way.

The Pitchfork

Of all implements, the pitchfork was the one
That came near to an imagined perfection:
When he tightened his raised hand and aimed with it,
It felt like a javelin, accurate and light.

So whether he played the warrior or the athlete
Or worked in earnest in the chaff and sweat,
He loved its grain of tapering, dark-flecked ash
Grown satiny from its own natural polish.

Riveted steel, turned timber, burnish, grain,
Smoothness, straightness, roundness, length and sheen.
Sweat-cured, sharpened, balanced, tested, fitted.
The springiness, the clip and dart of it.

And then when he thought of probes that reached the
        farthest,
He would see the shaft of a pitchfork sailing past
Evenly, imperturbably through space,
Its prongs starlit and absolutely soundless—

But has learned at last to follow that simple lead
Past its own aim, out to an other side
Where perfection—or nearness to it—is imagined
Not in the aiming but the opening hand.

The Settle Bed

Willed down, waited for, in place at last and for good.
Trunk-hasped, cart-heavy, painted an ignorant brown.
And pew-strait, bin-deep, standing four-square as an ark.

If I lie in it, I am cribbed in seasoned deal
Dry as the unkindled boards of a funeral ship.
My measure has been taken, my ear shuttered up.

Yet I hear an old sombre tide awash in the headboard:
Unpathetic *och ochs* and *och hohs*, the long bedtime
Sigh-life of Ulster, unwilling, unbeaten,

Protestant, Catholic, the Bible, the beads,
Long talks at gables by moonlight, boots on the hearth,
The small hours chimed sweetly away so next thing it was

The cock on the ridge-tiles.
                         And now this is 'an inheritance'—
Upright, rudimentary, unshiftably planked
In the long ago, yet willable forward

Again and again and again, cargoed with
Its own dumb, tongue-and-groove worthiness
And un-get-roundable weight. But to conquer that weight,

Imagine a dower of settle beds tumbled from heaven
Like some nonsensical vengeance come on the people,
Then learn from that harmless barrage that whatever is given

Can always be reimagined, however four-square,
Plank-thick, hull-stupid and out of its time
It happens to be. You are free as the lookout,

That far-seeing joker posted high over the fog,
Who declared by the time that he had got himself down
The actual ship had stolen away from beneath him.

from *Glanmore Revisited*

I. Scrabble

in memoriam Tom Delaney, archaeologist

Bare flags. Pump water. Winter-evening cold.
Our backs might never warm up but our faces
Burned from the hearth-blaze and the hot whiskeys.
It felt remembered even then, an old
Rightness half-imagined or foretold,
As green sticks hissed and spat into the ashes
And whatever rampaged out there couldn't reach us,
Firelit, shuttered, slated and stone-walled.

Year after year, our game of Scrabble: love
Taken for granted like any other word
That was chanced on and allowed within the rules.
So 'scrabble' let it be. Intransitive.
Meaning to scratch or rake at something hard.
Which is what he hears. Our scraping, clinking tools.

II. *The Cot*

Scythe and axe and hedge-clippers, the shriek
Of the gate the children used to swing on,
Poker, scuttle, tongs, a gravel rake—
The old activity starts up again
But starts up differently. We're on our own
Years later in the same *locus amoenus*,
Tenants no longer, but in full possession
Of an emptied house and whatever keeps between us.

Which must be more than keepsakes, even though
The child's cot's back in place where Catherine
Woke in the dawn and answered *doodle doo*
To the rooster in the farm across the road—
And is the same cot I myself slept in
When the whole world was a farm that eked and crowed.

V. *Lustral Sonnet*

Breaking and entering: from early on
Words that thrilled me far more than they scared me—
Even when I'd 'come into my own'
And owned a house, a man of property
Who lacked the proper outlook. I would never
Double-bar the door or lock the gate
Or draw the blinds or pull the curtains over
Or give 'security' a second thought.

But all changed when I took possession here
And had the old bed sawn on my instruction
Since the only way to move it down the stair
Was to cut the frame in two. A bad action,
So Greek with consequence, so dangerous,
Only pure words and deeds secure the house.

VII. *The Skylight*

You were the one for skylights. I opposed
Cutting into the seasoned tongue-and-groove
Of pitch pine. I liked it low and closed,
Its claustrophobic, nest-up-in-the-roof
Effect. I liked the snuff-dry feeling,
The perfect, trunk-lid fit of the old ceiling.
Under there, it was all hutch and hatch.
The blue slates kept the heat like midnight thatch.

But when the slates came off, extravagant
Sky entered and held surprise wide open.
For days I felt like an inhabitant
Of that house where the man sick of the palsy
Was lowered through the roof, had his sins forgiven,
Was healed, took up his bed and walked away.

A Pillowed Head

Matutinal. Mother-of-pearl
Summer come early. Slashed carmines
And washed milky blues.

To be first on the road,
Up with the ground-mists and pheasants.
To be older and grateful

That this time you too were half-grateful
The pangs had begun—prepared
And clear-headed, foreknowing

The trauma, entering on it
With full consent of the will.
(The first time, dismayed and arrayed

In your cut-off white cotton gown,
You were more bride than earth-mother
Up on the stirrup-rigged bed,

Who were self-possessed now
To the point of a walk on the pier
Before you checked in.)

And then later on I half-fainted
When the little slapped palpable girl
Was handed to me; but as usual

Came to in two wide-open eyes
That had been dawned into farther
Than ever, and had outseen the last

Of all of those mornings of waiting
When your domed brow was one long held silence
And the dawn chorus anything but.

A Royal Prospect

On the day of their excursion up the Thames
To Hampton Court, they were nearly sunstruck.
She with her neck bared in a page-boy cut,
He all dreamy anyhow, wild for her
But pretending to be a thousand miles away,
Studying the boat's wake in the water.
And here are the photographs. Head to one side,
In her sleeveless blouse, one bare shoulder high
And one arm loose, a bird with a dropped wing
Surprised in cover. He looks at you straight,
Assailable, enamoured, full of vows,
Young dauphin in the once-upon-a-time.
And next the lowish red-brick Tudor frontage.
No more photographs, however, now
We are present there as the smell of grass
And suntan oil, standing like their sixth sense
Behind them at the entrance to the maze,
Heartbroken for no reason, willing them
To dare it to the centre they are lost for . . .
Instead, like reflections staggered through warped glass,
They reappear as in a black and white
Old grainy newsreel, where their pleasure-boat
Goes back spotlit across sunken bridges
And they alone are borne downstream unscathed,
Between mud banks where the wounded rave all night
At flameless blasts and echoless gunfire—
In all of which is ominously figured
Their free passage through historic times,
Like a silk train being brushed across a leper
Or the safe conduct of two royal favourites,
Unhindered and resented and bright-eyed.
So let them keep a tally of themselves
And be accountable when called upon
For although by every golden mean their lot
Is fair and due, pleas will be allowed

Against every right and title vested in them
(And in a court where mere innocuousness
Has never gained approval or acquittal).

Wheels within Wheels

I

The first real grip I ever got on things
Was when I learned the art of pedalling
(By hand) a bike turned upside down, and drove
Its back wheel preternaturally fast.
I loved the disappearance of the spokes,
The way the space between the hub and rim
Hummed with transparency. If you threw
A potato into it, the hooped air
Spun mush and drizzle back into your face;
If you touched it with a straw, the straw frittered.
Something about the way those pedal treads
Worked very palpably at first against you
And then began to sweep your hand ahead
Into a new momentum—that all entered me
Like an access of free power, as if belief
Caught up and spun the objects of belief
In an orbit coterminous with longing.

II

But enough was not enough. Who ever saw
The limit in the given anyhow?
In fields beyond our house there was a well
('The well' we called it. It was more a hole
With water in it, with small hawthorn trees
On one side, and a muddy, dungy ooze
On the other, all tramped through by cattle).
I loved that too. I loved the turbid smell,
The sump-life of the place like old chain oil.
And there, next thing, I brought my bicycle.
I stood its saddle and its handlebars
Into the soft bottom, I touched the tyres

To the water's surface, then turned the pedals
Until like a mill-wheel pouring at the treadles
(But here reversed and lashing a mare's tail)
The world-refreshing and immersed back wheel
Spun lace and dirt-suds there before my eyes
And showered me in my own regenerate clays.
For weeks I made a nimbus of old glit.
Then the hub jammed, rims rusted, the chain snapped.

III

Nothing rose to the occasion after that
Until, in a circus ring, drumrolled and spotlit,
Cowgirls wheeled in, each one immaculate
At the still centre of a lariat.
Perpetuum mobile. Sheer pirouette.
Tumblers. Jongleurs. Ring-a-rosies. *Stet!*

Fosterling

'That heavy greenness fostered by water'
—JOHN MONTAGUE

At school I loved one picture's heavy greenness—
Horizons rigged with windmills' arms and sails.
The millhouses' still outlines. Their in-placeness
Still more in place when mirrored in canals.
I can't remember not ever having known
The immanent hydraulics of a land
Of *glar* and *glit* and floods at *dailigone*.
My silting hope. My lowlands of the mind.

Heaviness of being. And poetry
Sluggish in the doldrums of what happens.
Me waiting until I was nearly fifty
To credit marvels. Like the tree-clock of tin cans
The tinkers made. So long for air to brighten,
Time to be dazzled and the heart to lighten.

from *Squarings*

Lightenings

i

Shifting brilliancies. Then winter light
In a doorway, and on the stone doorstep
A beggar shivering in silhouette.

So the particular judgement might be set:
Bare wallstead and a cold hearth rained into—
Bright puddle where the soul-free cloud-life roams.

And after the commanded journey, what?
Nothing magnificent, nothing unknown.
A gazing out from far away, alone.

And it is not particular at all,
Just old truth dawning: there is no next-time-round.
Unroofed scope. Knowledge-freshening wind.

ii

Roof it again. Batten down. Dig in.
Drink out of tin. Know the scullery cold,
A latch, a door-bar, forged tongs and a grate.

Touch the crossbeam, drive iron in a wall,
Hang a line to verify the plumb
From lintel, coping-stone and chimney-breast.

Relocate the bedrock in the threshold.
Take squarings from the recessed gable pane.
Make your study the unregarded floor.

Sink every impulse like a bolt. Secure
The bastion of sensation. Do not waver
Into language. Do not waver in it.

iii

Squarings? In the game of marbles, squarings
Were all those anglings, aimings, feints and squints
You were allowed before you'd shoot, all those

Hunkerings, tensings, pressures of the thumb,
Test-outs and pull-backs, re-envisagings,
All the ways your arms kept hoping towards

Blind certainties that were going to prevail
Beyond the one-off moment of the pitch.
A million million accuracies passed

Between your muscles' outreach and that space
Marked with three round holes and a drawn line.
You squinted out from a skylight of the world.

Three marble holes thumbed in the concrete road
Before the concrete hardened still remained
Three decades after the marble-player vanished

Into Australia. Three stops to play
The music of the arbitrary on.
Blow on them now and hear an undersong

Your levelled breath made once going over
The empty bottle. Improvise. Make free
Like old hay in its flimsy afterlife

High on a windblown hedge. Ocarina earth.
Three listening posts up on some hard-baked tier
Above the resonating amphorae.

vi

Once, as a child, out in a field of sheep,
Thomas Hardy pretended to be dead
And lay down flat among their dainty shins.

In that sniffed-at, bleated-into, grassy space
He experimented with infinity.
His small cool brow was like an anvil waiting

For sky to make it sing the perfect pitch
Of his dumb being, and that stir he caused
In the fleece-hustle was the original

Of a ripple that would travel eighty years
Outward from there, to be the same ripple
Inside him at its last circumference.

vii

(I misremembered. He went down on all fours,
Florence Emily says, crossing a ewe-leaze.
Hardy sought the creatures face to face,

Their witless eyes and liability
To panic made him feel less alone,
Made proleptic sorrow stand a moment

Over him, perfectly known and sure.
And then the flock's dismay went swimming on
Into the blinks and murmurs and deflections

He'd know at parties in renowned old age
When sometimes he imagined himself a ghost
And circulated with that new perspective.)

viii

The annals say: when the monks of Clonmacnoise
Were all at prayers inside the oratory
A ship appeared above them in the air.

The anchor dragged along behind so deep
It hooked itself into the altar rails
And then, as the big hull rocked to a standstill,

A crewman shinned and grappled down the rope
And struggled to release it. But in vain.
'This man can't bear our life here and will drown,'

The abbot said, 'unless we help him.' So
They did, the freed ship sailed, and the man climbed back
Out of the marvellous as he had known it.

ix

A boat that did not rock or wobble once
Sat in long grass one Sunday afternoon
In nineteen forty-one or -two. The heat

Out on Lough Neagh and in where cattle stood
Jostling and skittering near the hedge
Grew redolent of the tweed skirt and tweed sleeve

I nursed on. I remember little treble
Timber-notes their smart heels struck from planks,
Me cradled in an elbow like a secret

Open now as the eye of heaven was then
Above three sisters talking, talking steady
In a boat the ground still falls and falls from under.

x

Overhang of grass and seedling birch
On the quarry face. Rock-hob where you watched
All that cargoed brightness travelling

Above and beyond and sumptuously across
The water in its clear deep dangerous holes
On the quarry floor. Ultimate

Fathomableness, ultimate
Stony up-againstness: could you reconcile
What was diaphanous there with what was massive?

Were you equal to or were you opposite
To build-ups so promiscuous and weightless?
Shield your eyes, look up and face the music.

xii

And lightening? One meaning of that
Beyond the usual sense of alleviation,
Illumination, and so on, is this:

A phenomenal instant when the spirit flares
With pure exhilaration before death—
The good thief in us harking to the promise!

So paint him on Christ's right hand, on a promontory
Scanning empty space, so body-racked he seems
Untranslatable into the bliss

Ached for at the moon-rim of his forehead,
By nail-craters on the dark side of his brain:
This day thou shalt be with Me in Paradise.

Settings

Hazel stealth. A trickle in the culvert.
Athletic sealight on the doorstep slab,
On the sea itself, on silent roofs and gables.

Whitewashed suntraps. Hedges hot as chimneys.
Chairs on all fours. A plate-rack braced and laden.
The fossil poetry of hob and slate.

Desire within its moat, dozing at ease—
Like a gorged cormorant on the rock at noon,
Exiled and in tune with the big glitter.

Re-enter this as the adult of solitude,
The silence-forder and the definite
Presence you sensed withdrawing first time round.

xiv

One afternoon I was seraph on gold leaf.
I stood on the railway sleepers hearing larks,
Grasshoppers, cuckoos, dog-barks, trainer planes

Cutting and modulating and drawing off.
Heat wavered on the immaculate line
And shine of the cogged rails. On either side,

Dog daisies stood like vestals, the hot stones
Were clover-meshed and streaked with engine oil.
Air spanned, passage waited, the balance rode,

Nothing prevailed, whatever was in store
Witnessed itself already taking place
In a time marked by assent and by hiatus.

xv

And strike this scene in gold too, in relief,
So that a greedy eye cannot exhaust it:
Stable straw, Rembrandt-gleam and burnish

Where my father bends to a tea-chest packed with salt,
The hurricane lamp held up at eye-level
In his bunched left fist, his right hand foraging

For the unbleeding, vivid-fleshed bacon,
Home-cured hocks pulled up into the light
For pondering a while and putting back.

That night I owned the piled grain of Egypt.
I watched the sentry's torchlight on the hoard.
I stood in the door, unseen and blazed upon.

xix

Memory as a building or a city,
Well lighted, well laid out, appointed with
Tableaux vivants and costumed effigies—

Statues in purple cloaks, or painted red,
Ones wearing crowns, ones smeared with mud or blood:
So that the mind's eye could haunt itself

With fixed associations and learn to read
Its own contents in meaningful order,
Ancient textbooks recommended that

Familiar places be linked deliberately
With a code of images. You knew the portent
In each setting, you blinked and concentrated.

xxii

Where does spirit live? Inside or outside
Things remembered, made things, things unmade?
What came first, the seabird's cry or the soul

Imagined in the dawn cold when it cried?
Where does it roost at last? On dungy sticks
In a jackdaw's nest up in the old stone tower

Or a marble bust commanding the parterre?
How habitable is perfected form?
And how inhabited the windy light?

What's the use of a held note or held line
That cannot be assailed for reassurance?
(Set questions for the ghost of W.B.)

xxiv

Deserted harbour stillness. Every stone
Clarified and dormant under water,
The harbour wall a masonry of silence.

Fullness. Shimmer. Laden high Atlantic
The moorings barely stirred in, very slight
Clucking of the swell against boat boards.

Perfected vision: cockle minarets
Consigned down there with green-slicked bottle glass,
Shell-debris and a reddened bud of sandstone.

Air and ocean known as antecedents
Of each other. In apposition with
Omnipresence, equilibrium, brim.

Crossings

Everything flows. Even a solid man,
A pillar to himself and to his trade,
All yellow boots and stick and soft felt hat,

Can sprout wings at the ankle and grow fleet
As the god of fair days, stone posts, roads and crossroads,
Guardian of travellers and psychopomp.

'Look for a man with an ashplant on the boat,'
My father told his sister setting out
For London, 'and stay near him all night

And you'll be safe.' Flow on, flow on
The journey of the soul with its soul guide
And the mysteries of dealing-men with sticks!

xxix

Scissor-and-slap abruptness of a latch.
Its coldness to the thumb. Its see-saw lift
And drop and innocent harshness.

Which is a music of binding and of loosing
Unheard in this generation, but there to be
Called up or called down at a touch renewed.

Once the latch pronounces, roof
Is original again, threshold fatal,
The sanction powerful as the foreboding.

Your footstep is already known, so bow
Just a little, raise your right hand,
Make impulse one with wilfulness, and enter.

XXX

On St Brigid's Day the new life could be entered
By going through her girdle of straw rope:
The proper way for men was right leg first,

Then right arm and right shoulder, head, then left
Shoulder, arm and leg. Women drew it down
Over the body and stepped out of it.

The open they came into by these moves
Stood opener, hoops came off the world,
They could feel the February air

Still soft above their heads and imagine
The limp rope fray and flare like wind-borne gleanings
Or an unhindered goldfinch over ploughland.

xxxii

Running water never disappointed.
Crossing water always furthered something.
Stepping stones were stations of the soul.

A kesh could mean the track some called a *causey*
Raised above the wetness of the bog,
Or the causey where it bridged old drains and streams.

It steadies me to tell these things. Also
I cannot mention keshes or the ford
Without my father's shade appearing to me

On a path towards sunset, eyeing spades and clothes
That turf-cutters stowed perhaps or souls cast off
Before they crossed the log that spans the burn.

xxxiii

Be literal a moment. Recollect
Walking out on what had been emptied out
After he died, turning your back and leaving.

That morning tiles were harder, windows colder,
The raindrops on the pane more scourged, the grass
Barer to the sky, more wind-harrowed,

Or so it seemed. The house that he had planned
'Plain, big, straight, ordinary, you know',
A paradigm of rigour and correction,

Rebuke to fanciness and shrine to limit,
Stood firmer than ever for its own idea
Like a printed X-ray for the X-rayed body.

xxxiv

Yeats said, *To those who see spirits, human skin*
For a long time afterwards appears most coarse.
The face I see that all falls short of since

Passes down an aisle: I share the bus
From San Francisco Airport into Berkeley
With one other passenger, who's dropped

At the Treasure Island military base
Half-way across Bay Bridge. Vietnam-bound,
He could have been one of the newly dead come back,

Unsurprisable but still disappointed,
Having to bear his farm-boy self again,
His shaving cuts, his otherworldly brow.

xxxvi

And yes, my friend, we too walked through a valley.
Once. In darkness. With all the streetlamps off.
As danger gathered and the march dispersed.

Scene from Dante, made more memorable
By one of his head-clearing similes—
Fireflies, say, since the policemen's torches

Clustered and flicked and tempted us to trust
Their unpredictable, attractive light.
We were like herded shades who had to cross

And did cross, in a panic, to the car
Parked as we'd left it, that gave when we got in
Like Charon's boat under the faring poets.

Squarings

In famous poems by the sage Han Shan,
Cold Mountain is a place that can also mean
A state of mind. Or different states of mind

At different times, for the poems seem
One-off, impulsive, the kind of thing that starts
I have sat here facing the Cold Mountain

For twenty-nine years, or *There is no path
That goes all the way*—enviable stuff,
Unfussy and believable.

Talking about it isn't good enough
But quoting from it at least demonstrates
The virtue of an art that knows its mind.

xxxviii

We climbed the Capitol by moonlight, felt
The transports of temptation on the heights:
We were privileged and belated and we knew it.

Then something in me moved to prophesy
Against the beloved stand-offishness of marble
And all emulation of stone-cut verses.

'Down with form triumphant, long live,' (said I)
'Form mendicant and convalescent. We attend
The come-back of pure water and the prayer-wheel.'

To which a voice replied, 'Of course we do.
But the others are in the Forum Café waiting,
Wondering where we are. What'll you have?'

When you sat, far-eyed and cold, in the basalt throne
Of 'the wishing chair' at Giant's Causeway,
The small of your back made very solid sense.

Like a papoose at sap-time strapped to a maple tree,
You gathered force out of the world-tree's hardness.
If you stretched your hand forth, things might turn to stone.

But you were only goose-fleshed skin and bone,
The rocks and wonder of the world were only
Lava crystallized, salts of the earth

The wishing chair gave a savour to, its kelp
And ozone freshening your outlook
Beyond the range you thought you'd settled for.

xl

I was four but I turned four hundred maybe
Encountering the ancient dampish feel
Of a clay floor. Maybe four thousand even.

Anyhow, there it was. Milk poured for cats
In a rank puddle-place, splash-darkened mould
Around the terracotta water-crock.

Ground of being. Body's deep obedience
To all its shifting tenses. A half-door
Opening directly into starlight.

Out of that earth house I inherited
A stack of singular, cold memory-weights
To load me, hand and foot, in the scale of things.

xli

Sand-bed, they said. And gravel-bed. Before
I knew river shallows or river pleasures
I knew the ore of longing in those words.

The places I go back to have not failed
But will not last. Waist-deep in cow-parsley,
I re-enter the swim, riding or quelling

The very currents memory is composed of,
Everything accumulated ever
As I took squarings from the tops of bridges

Or the banks of self at evening.
Lick of fear. Sweet transience. Flirt and splash.
Crumpled flow the sky-dipped willows trailed in.

xlii

Heather and kesh and turf stacks reappear
Summer by summer still, grasshoppers and all,
The same yet rarer: fields of the nearly blessed

Where gaunt ones in their shirtsleeves stooped and dug
Or stood alone at dusk surveying bog-banks—
Apparitions now, yet active still

And territorial, still sure of their ground,
Still interested, not knowing how far
The country of the shades has been pushed back,

How long the lark has stopped outside these fields
And only seems unstoppable to them
Caught like a far hill in a freak of sunshine.

xliii

Choose one set of tracks and track a hare
Until the prints stop, just like that, in snow.
End of the line. Smooth drifts. Where did she go?

Back on her tracks, of course, then took a spring
Yards off to the side; clean break; no scent or sign.
She landed in her form and ate the snow.

Consider too the ancient hieroglyph
Of 'hare and zig-zag', which meant 'to exist',
To be on the *qui vive*, weaving and dodging

Like our friend who sprang (goodbye) beyond our ken
And missed a round at last (but of course he'd stood it):
The shake-the-heart, the dew-hammer, the far-eyed.

xliv

All gone into the world of light? Perhaps
As we read the line sheer forms do crowd
The starry vestibule. Otherwise

They do not. What lucency survives
Is blanched as worms on nightlines I would lift,
Ungratified if always well prepared

For the nothing there—which was only what had been there.
Although in fact it is more like a caught line snapping,
That moment of admission of *All gone*,

When the rod butt loses touch and the tip drools
And eddies swirl a dead leaf past in silence
Swifter (it seems) than the water's passage.

xlv

For certain ones what was written may come true:
They shall live on in the distance
At the mouths of rivers.

For our ones, no. They will re-enter
Dryness that was heaven on earth to them,
Happy to eat the scones baked out of clay.

For some, perhaps, the delta's reed-beds
And cold bright-footed seabirds always wheeling.
For our ones, snuff

And hob-soot and the heat off ashes.
And a judge who comes between them and the sun
In a pillar of radiant house-dust.

xlvi

Mountain air from the mountain up behind;
Out front, the end-of-summer, stone-walled fields;
And in a slated house the fiddle going

Like a flat stone skimmed at sunset
Or the irrevocable slipstream of flat earth
Still fleeing behind space.

Was music once a proof of God's existence?
As long as it admits things beyond measure,
That supposition stands.

So let the ear attend like a farmhouse window
In placid light, where the extravagant
Passed once under full sail into the longed-for.

xlvii

The visible sea at a distance from the shore
Or beyond the anchoring grounds
Was called the offing.

The emptier it stood, the more compelled
The eye that scanned it.
But once you turned your back on it, your back

Was suddenly all eyes like Argus's.
Then, when you'd look again, the offing felt
Untrespassed still, and yet somehow vacated

As if a lambent troop that exercised
On the borders of your vision had withdrawn
Behind the skyline to manoeuvre and regroup.

xlviii

Strange how things in the offing, once they're sensed,
Convert to things foreknown;
And how what's come upon is manifest

Only in light of what has been gone through.
Seventh heaven may be
The whole truth of a sixth sense come to pass.

At any rate, when light breaks over me
The way it did on the road beyond Coleraine
Where wind got saltier, the sky more hurried

And silver lamé shivered on the Bann
Out in mid-channel between the painted poles,
That day I'll be in step with what escaped me.

A Transgression

The teacher let some big boys out at two
    To gather sticks
  (In scanty nineteen forty-six)
And even though I never was supposed to

I wanted out as well. One afternoon
    I raised my hand
  With those free livers off the land
And found myself at large an hour too soon

Under a raggedy, hurrying sky
    On the road home.
  If ever I felt 'heaven's dome'
Was what I lived beneath, it was that day

I lied myself into my own desire,
    Displaced, afraid
  At what I'd dared to be ahead
Of time. The black spot where the gypsies' fire

Had charred the roadside grass, the rags that blew
    On the stripped hedge,
  The cold—it put me all on edge.
Escape-joy died, one magpie rose and flew

And left an emptiness I walked on through
    To come down to earth
  In my parents' gaze, the whole question of worth,
And their knowledge that loved on without ado.

FROM

The Spirit Level

[1 9 9 6]

The Rain Stick

for Beth and Rand

Up-end the rain stick and what happens next
Is a music that you never would have known
To listen for. In a cactus stalk

Downpour, sluice-rush, spillage and backwash
Come flowing through. You stand there like a pipe
Being played by water, you shake it again lightly

And diminuendo runs through all its scales
Like a gutter stopping trickling. And now here comes
A sprinkle of drops out of the freshened leaves,

Then subtle little wets off grass and daisies;
Then glitter-drizzle, almost-breaths of air.
Up-end the stick again. What happens next

Is undiminished for having happened once,
Twice, ten, a thousand times before.
Who cares if all the music that transpires

Is the fall of grit or dry seeds through a cactus?
You are like a rich man entering heaven
Through the ear of a raindrop. Listen now again.

Mint

It looked like a clump of small dusty nettles
Growing wild at the gable of the house
Beyond where we dumped our refuse and old bottles:
Unverdant ever, almost beneath notice.

But, to be fair, it also spelled promise
And newness in the back yard of our life
As if something callow yet tenacious
Sauntered in green alleys and grew rife.

The snip of scissor blades, the light of Sunday
Mornings when the mint was cut and loved:
My last things will be first things slipping from me.
Yet let all things go free that have survived.

Let the smells of mint go heady and defenceless
Like inmates liberated in that yard.
Like the disregarded ones we turned against
Because we'd failed them by our disregard.

A Sofa in the Forties

All of us on the sofa in a line, kneeling
Behind each other, eldest down to youngest,
Elbows going like pistons, for this was a train

And between the jamb-wall and the bedroom door
Our speed and distance were inestimable.
First we shunted, then we whistled, then

Somebody collected the invisible
For tickets and very gravely punched it
As carriage after carriage under us

Moved faster, *chooka-chook*, the sofa legs
Went giddy and the unreachable ones
Far out on the kitchen floor began to wave.

    *

Ghost-train? Death-gondola? The carved, curved ends,
Black leatherette and ornate gauntness of it
Made it seem the sofa had achieved

Flotation. Its castors on tiptoe,
Its braid and fluent backboard gave it airs
Of superannuated pageantry:

When visitors endured it, straight-backed,
When it stood off in its own remoteness,
When the insufficient toys appeared on it

On Christmas mornings, it held out as itself,
Potentially heavenbound, earthbound for sure,
Among things that might add up or let you down.

    *

We entered history and ignorance
Under the wireless shelf. *Yippee-i-ay*,
Sang 'The Riders of the Range'. HERE IS THE NEWS,

Said the absolute speaker. Between him and us
A great gulf was fixed where pronunciation
Reigned tyrannically. The aerial wire

Swept from a treetop down in through a hole
Bored in the windowframe. When it moved in wind,
The sway of language and its furtherings

Swept and swayed in us like nets in water
Or the abstract, lonely curve of distant trains
As we entered history and ignorance.

    *

We occupied our seats with all our might,
Fit for the uncomfortableness.
Constancy was its own reward already.

Out in front, on the big upholstered arm,
Somebody craned to the side, driver or
Fireman, wiping his dry brow with the air

Of one who had run the gauntlet. We were
The last thing on his mind, it seemed; we sensed
A tunnel coming up where we'd pour through

Like unlit carriages through fields at night,
Our only job to sit, eyes straight ahead,
And be transported and make engine noise.

Keeping Going

for Hugh

The piper coming from far away is you
With a whitewash brush for a sporran
Wobbling round you, a kitchen chair
Upside down on your shoulder, your right arm
Pretending to tuck the bag beneath your elbow,
Your pop-eyes and big cheeks nearly bursting
With laughter, but keeping the drone going on
Interminably, between catches of breath.

*

The whitewash brush. An old blanched skirted thing
On the back of the byre door, biding its time
Until spring airs spelled lime in a work-bucket
And a potstick to mix it in with water.
Those smells brought tears to the eyes, we inhaled
A kind of greeny burning and thought of brimstone.
But the slop of the actual job
Of brushing walls, the watery grey
Being lashed on in broad swatches, then drying out
Whiter and whiter, all that worked like magic.
Where had we come from, what was this kingdom
We knew we'd been restored to? Our shadows
Moved on the wall and a tar border glittered
The full length of the house, a black divide
Like a freshly opened, pungent, reeking trench.

*

Piss at the gable, the dead will congregate.
But separately. The women after dark,
Hunkering there a moment before bedtime,
The only time the soul was let alone,
The only time that face and body calmed
In the eye of heaven.
                    Buttermilk and urine,

The pantry, the housed beasts, the listening bedroom.
We were all together there in a foretime,
In a knowledge that might not translate beyond
Those wind-heaved midnights we still cannot be sure
Happened or not. It smelled of hill-fort clay
And cattle dung. When the thorn tree was cut down
You broke your arm. I shared the dread
When a strange bird perched for days on the byre roof.

*

That scene, with Macbeth helpless and desperate
In his nightmare—when he meets the hags again
And sees the apparitions in the pot—
I felt at home with that one all right. Hearth,
Steam and ululation, the smoky hair
Curtaining a cheek. 'Don't go near bad boys
In that college that you're bound for. Do you hear me?
Do you hear me speaking to you? Don't forget!'
And then the potstick quickening the gruel,
The steam crown swirled, everything intimate
And fear-swathed brightening for a moment,
Then going dull and fatal and away.

*

Grey matter like gruel flecked with blood
In spatters on the whitewash. A clean spot
Where his head had been, other stains subsumed
In the parched wall he leant his back against
That morning like any other morning,
Part-time reservist, toting his lunch-box.
A car came slow down Castle Street, made the halt,
Crossed the Diamond, slowed again and stopped
Level with him, although it was not his lift.
And then he saw an ordinary face
For what it was and a gun in his own face.
His right leg was hooked back, his sole and heel
Against the wall, his right knee propped up steady,
So he never moved, just pushed with all his might
Against himself, then fell past the tarred strip,
Feeding the gutter with his copious blood.

*

My dear brother, you have good stamina.
You stay on where it happens. Your big tractor
Pulls up at the Diamond, you wave at people,
You shout and laugh above the revs, you keep
Old roads open by driving on the new ones.
You called the piper's sporrans whitewash brushes
And then dressed up and marched us through the kitchen,
But you cannot make the dead walk or right wrong.
I see you at the end of your tether sometimes,
In the milking parlour, holding yourself up
Between two cows until your turn goes past,
Then coming to in the smell of dung again
And wondering, is this all? As it was
In the beginning, is now and shall be?
Then rubbing your eyes and seeing our old brush
Up on the byre door, and keeping going.

Two Lorries

It's raining on black coal and warm wet ashes.
There are tyre-marks in the yard, Agnew's old lorry
Has all its cribs down and Agnew the coalman
With his Belfast accent's sweet-talking my mother.
Would she ever go to a film in Magherafelt?
But it's raining and he still has half the load

To deliver farther on. This time the lode
Our coal came from was silk-black, so the ashes
Will be the silkiest white. The Magherafelt
(Via Toomebridge) bus goes by. The half-stripped lorry
With its emptied, folded coal-bags moves my mother:
The tasty ways of a leather-aproned coalman!

And films no less! The conceit of a coalman . . .
She goes back in and gets out the black lead
And emery paper, this nineteen-forties mother,
All business round her stove, half-wiping ashes
With a backhand from her cheek as the bolted lorry
Gets revved and turned and heads for Magherafelt

And the last delivery. Oh, Magherafelt!
Oh, dream of red plush and a city coalman
As time fastforwards and a different lorry
Groans into shot, up Broad Street, with a payload
That will blow the bus station to dust and ashes . . .
After that happened, I'd a vision of my mother,

A revenant on the bench where I would meet her
In that cold-floored waiting-room in Magherafelt,
Her shopping bags full up with shovelled ashes.
Death walked out past her like a dust-faced coalman
Refolding body-bags, plying his load
Empty upon empty, in a flurry

Of motes and engine-revs, but which lorry
Was it now? Young Agnew's or that other,
Heavier, deadlier one, set to explode
In a time beyond her time in Magherafelt . . .
So tally bags and sweet-talk darkness, coalman.
Listen to the rain spit in new ashes

As you heft a load of dust that was Magherafelt,
Then reappear from your lorry as my mother's
Dreamboat coalman filmed in silk-white ashes.

Damson

Gules and cement dust. A matte tacky blood
On the bricklayer's knuckles, like the damson stain
That seeped through his packed lunch.
                                    A full hod stood
Against the mortared wall, his big bright trowel
In his left hand (for once) was pointing down
As he marvelled at his right, held high and raw:
King of the castle, scaffold-stepper, shown
Bleeding to the world.
                        Wound that I saw
In glutinous colour fifty years ago—
Damson as omen, weird, a dream to read—
Is weeping with the held-at-arm's-length dead
From everywhere and nowhere, here and now.

        *

Over and over, the slur, the scrape and mix
As he trowelled and retrowelled and laid down
Courses of glum mortar. Then the bricks
Jiggled and settled, tocked and tapped in line.
I loved especially the trowel's shine,
Its edge and apex always coming clean
And brightening itself by mucking in.
It looked light but felt heavy as a weapon,
Yet when he lifted it there was no strain.
It was all point and skim and float and glisten
Until he washed and lapped it tight in sacking
Like a cult blade that had to be kept hidden.

        *

Ghosts with their tongues out for a lick of blood
Are crowding up the ladder, all unhealed,
And some of them still rigged in bloody gear.
Drive them back to the doorstep or the road

Where they lay in their own blood once, in the hot
Nausea and last gasp of dear life.
Trowel-wielder, woundie, drive them off
Like Odysseus in Hades lashing out
With his sword that dug the trench and cut the throat
Of the sacrificial lamb.
                              But not like him—
Builder, not sacker, your shield the mortar board—
Drive them back to the wine-dark taste of home,
The smell of damsons simmering in a pot,
Jam ladled thick and steaming down the sunlight.

Weighing In

The 56 lb. weight. A solid iron
Unit of negation. Stamped and cast
With an inset, rung-thick, moulded, short crossbar

For a handle. Squared-off and harmless-looking
Until you tried to lift it, then a socket-ripping,
Life-belittling force—

Gravity's black box, the immovable
Stamp and squat and square-root of dead weight.
Yet balance it

Against another one placed on a weighbridge—
On a well-adjusted, freshly greased weighbridge—
And everything trembled, flowed with give and take.

      *

And this is all the good tidings amount to:
This principle of bearing, bearing up
And bearing out, just having to

Balance the intolerable in others
Against our own, having to abide
Whatever we settled for and settled into

Against our better judgement. Passive
Suffering makes the world go round.
Peace on earth, men of good will, all that

Holds good only as long as the balance holds,
The scales ride steady and the angels' strain
Prolongs itself at an unearthly pitch.

      *

To refuse the other cheek. To cast the stone.
Not to do so some time, not to break with
The obedient one you hurt yourself into

Is to fail the hurt, the self, the ingrown rule.
Prophesy who struck thee! When soldiers mocked
Blindfolded Jesus and he didn't strike back

They were neither shamed nor edified, although
Something was made manifest—the power
Of power not exercised, of hope inferred

By the powerless forever. Still, for Jesus' sake,
Do me a favour, would you, just this once?
Prophesy, give scandal, cast the stone.

*

Two sides to every question, yes, yes, yes . . .
But every now and then, just weighing in
Is what it must come down to, and without

Any self-exculpation or self-pity.
Alas, one night when follow-through was called for
And a quick hit would have fairly rankled,

You countered that it was my narrowness
That kept me keen, so got a first submission.
I held back when I should have drawn blood

And that way (*mea culpa*) lost an edge.
A deep mistaken chivalry, old friend.
At this stage only foul play cleans the slate.

St Kevin and the Blackbird

And then there was St Kevin and the blackbird.
The saint is kneeling, arms stretched out, inside
His cell, but the cell is narrow, so

One turned-up palm is out the window, stiff
As a crossbeam, when a blackbird lands
And lays in it and settles down to nest.

Kevin feels the warm eggs, the small breast, the tucked
Neat head and claws and, finding himself linked
Into the network of eternal life,

Is moved to pity: now he must hold his hand
Like a branch out in the sun and rain for weeks
Until the young are hatched and fledged and flown.

*

And since the whole thing's imagined anyhow,
Imagine being Kevin. Which is he?
Self-forgetful or in agony all the time

From the neck on out down through his hurting forearms?
Are his fingers sleeping? Does he still feel his knees?
Or has the shut-eyed blank of underearth

Crept up through him? Is there distance in his head?
Alone and mirrored clear in love's deep river,
'To labour and not to seek reward,' he prays,

A prayer his body makes entirely
For he has forgotten self, forgotten bird
And on the riverbank forgotten the river's name.

from *The Flight Path*

IV

The following for the record, in the light
Of everything before and since:
One bright May morning, nineteen seventy-nine,
Just off the 'red-eye special' from New York,
I'm on the train for Belfast. Plain, simple
Exhilaration at being back: the sea
At Skerries, the nuptial hawthorn bloom,
The trip north taking sweet hold like a chain
On every bodily sprocket.
                                       Enter then—
As if he were some *film noir* border guard—
Enter this one I'd last met in a dream,
More grimfaced now than in the dream itself
When he'd flagged me down at the side of a mountain road,
Come up and leant his elbow on the roof
And explained through the open window of the car
That all I'd have to do was drive a van
Carefully in to the next customs post
At Pettigo, switch off, get out as if
I were on my way with dockets to the office—
But then instead I'd walk ten yards more down
Towards the main street and get in with—here
Another schoolfriend's name, a wink and smile,
I'd know him all right, he'd be in a Ford
And I'd be home in three hours' time, as safe
As houses . . .
                       So he enters and sits down
Opposite and goes for me head on.
'When, for fuck's sake, are you going to write
Something for us?' 'If I do write something,
Whatever it is, I'll be writing for myself.'
And that was that. Or words to that effect.

385

The jail walls in those months were smeared with shite.
Out of Long Kesh after his dirty protest
The red eyes were the eyes of Ciaran Nugent
Like something out of Dante's scurfy hell,
Drilling their way through the rhymes and images
Where I too walked behind the righteous Virgil,
As safe as houses and translating freely:
When he had said all this, his eyes rolled
And his teeth, like a dog's teeth clamping round a bone,
Bit into the skull and again took hold.

      V

When I answered that I came from 'far away',
The policeman at the roadblock snapped, 'Where's that?'
He'd only half-heard what I said and thought
It was the name of some place up the country.

And now it is—both where I have been living
And where I left—a distance still to go
Like starlight that is light years on the go
From far away and takes light years arriving.

Mycenae Lookout

for Cynthia and Dimitri Hadzi

The ox is on my tongue.
—AESCHYLUS, *Agamemnon*

1. The Watchman's War

Some people wept, and not for sorrow—joy
That the king had armed and upped and sailed for Troy,
But inside me like struck sound in a gong
That killing-fest, the life-warp and world-wrong
It brought to pass, still augured and endured.
I'd dream of blood in bright webs in a ford,
Of bodies raining down like tattered meat
On top of me asleep—and me the lookout
The queen's command had posted and forgotten,
The blind spot her farsightedness relied on.
And then the ox would lurch against the gong
And deaden it and I would feel my tongue
Like the dropped gangplank of a cattle truck,
Trampled and rattled, running piss and muck,
All swimmy-trembly as the lick of fire,
A victory beacon in an abattoir . . .
Next thing then I would waken at a loss,
For all the world a sheepdog stretched in grass,
Exposed to what I knew, still honour-bound
To concentrate attention out beyond
The city and the border, on that line
Where the blaze would leap the hills when Troy had fallen.

My sentry work was fate, a home to go to,
An in-between-times that I had to row through
Year after year: when the mist would start
To lift off fields and inlets, when morning light
Would open like the grain of light being split,
Day in, day out, I'd come alive again,
Silent and sunned as an esker on a plain,

Up on my elbows, gazing, biding time
In my outpost on the roof . . . What was to come
Out of that ten years' wait that was the war
Flawed the black mirror of my frozen stare.
If a god of justice had reached down from heaven
For a strong beam to hang his scale-pans on
He would have found me tensed and ready-made.
I balanced between destiny and dread
And saw it coming, clouds bloodshot with the red
Of victory fires, the raw wound of that dawn
Igniting and erupting, bearing down
Like lava on a fleeing population . . .
Up on my elbows, head back, shutting out
The agony of Clytemnestra's love-shout
That rose through the palace like the yell of troops
Hurled by King Agamemnon from the ships.

2. Cassandra

No such thing
as innocent
bystanding.

Her soiled vest,
her little breasts,
her clipped, devast-

ated, scabbed
punk head,
the char-eyed

famine gawk—
she looked
camp-fucked

and simple.
People
could feel

a missed
trueness in them
focus,

a homecoming
in her dropped-wing,
half-calculating

bewilderment.
No such thing
as innocent.

Old King Cock-
of-the-Walk
was back,

King Kill-
the-Child-
and-Take-

What-Comes,
King Agamem-
non's drum-

balled, old buck's
stride was back.
And then her Greek

words came,
a lamb
at lambing time,

bleat of clair-
voyant dread,
the gene-hammer

and tread
of the roused god.
And the result-

ant shock desire
in bystanders
to do it to her

there and then.
Little rent
cunt of their guilt:

in she went
to the knife,
to the killer wife,

to the net over
her and her slaver,
the Troy reaver,

saying, 'A wipe
of the sponge,
that's it.

The shadow-hinge
swings unpredict-
ably and the light's

blanked out.'

3. His Dawn Vision

Cities of grass. Fort walls. The dumbstruck palace.
I'd come to with the night wind on my face,
Agog, alert again, but far, far less

Focused on victory than I should have been—
Still isolated in my old disdain
Of claques who always needed to be seen

And heard as the true Argives. Mouth athletes,
Quoting the oracle and quoting dates,
Petitioning, accusing, taking votes.

No element that should have carried weight
Out of the grievous distance would translate.
Our war stalled in the pre-articulate.

The little violets' heads bowed on their stems,
The pre-dawn gossamers, all dew and scrim
And star-lace, it was more through them

I felt the beating of the huge time-wound
We lived inside. My soul wept in my hand
When I would touch them, my whole being rained

Down on myself, I saw cities of grass,
Valleys of longing, tombs, a windswept brightness,
And far off, in a hilly, ominous place,

Small crowds of people watching as a man
Jumped a fresh earth-wall and another ran
Amorously, it seemed, to strike him down.

4. The Nights

They both needed to talk,
pretending what they needed
was my advice. Behind backs
each one of them confided
it was sexual overload
every time they did it—
and indeed from the beginning
(a child could have hardly missed it)
their real life was the bed.

The king should have been told,
but who was there to tell him
if not myself? I willed them
to cease and break the hold
of my cross-purposed silence
but still kept on, all smiles
to Aegisthus every morning,

much favoured and self-loathing.
The roof was like an eardrum.

The ox's tons of dumb
inertia stood, head-down
and motionless as a herm.
Atlas, watchmen's patron,
would come into my mind,
the only other one
up at all hours, ox-bowed
under his yoke of cloud
out there at the world's end.

The loft-floor where the gods
and goddesses took lovers
and made out endlessly
successfully, those thuds
and moans through the cloud cover
were wholly on his shoulders.
Sometimes I thought of us
apotheosized to boulders
called Aphrodite's Pillars.

High and low in those days
hit their stride together.
When the captains in the horse
felt Helen's hand caress
its wooden boards and belly
they nearly rode each other.
But in the end Troy's mothers
bore their brunt in alley,
bloodied cot and bed.
The war put all men mad,
horned, horsed or roof-posted,
the boasting and the bested.

My own mind was a bull-pen
where horned King Agamemnon
had stamped his weight in gold.

But when hills broke into flame
and the queen wailed on and came,
it was the king I sold.
I moved beyond bad faith:
for his bullion bars, his bonus
was a rope-net and a bloodbath.
And the peace had come upon us.

5. His Reverie of Water

At Troy, at Athens, what I most clearly
see and nearly smell
is the fresh water.

A filled bath, still unentered
and unstained, waiting behind housewalls
that the far cries of the butchered on the plain

keep dying into, until the hero comes
surging in incomprehensibly
to be attended to and be alone,

stripped to the skin, blood-plastered, moaning
and rocking, splashing, dozing off,
accommodated as if he were a stranger.

And the well at Athens too.
Or rather that old lifeline leading up
and down from the Acropolis

to the well itself, a set of timber steps
slatted in between the sheer cliff face
and a free-standing, covering spur of rock,

secret staircase the defenders knew
and the invaders found, where what was to be
Greek met Greek,

the ladder of the future
and the past, besieger and besieged,
the treadmill of assault

turned waterwheel, the rungs of stealth
and habit all the one
bare foot extended, searching.

And then this ladder of our own that ran
deep into a well-shaft being sunk
in broad daylight, men puddling at the source

through tawny mud, then coming back up
deeper in themselves for having been there,
like discharged soldiers testing the safe ground,

finders, keepers, seers of fresh water
in the bountiful round mouths of iron pumps
and gushing taps.

The Gravel Walks

River gravel. In the beginning, that.
High summer, and the angler's motorbike
Deep in roadside flowers, like a fallen knight
Whose ghost we'd lately questioned: 'Any luck?'

As the engines of the world prepared, green nuts
Dangled and clustered closer to the whirlpool.
The trees dipped down. The flints and sandstone-bits
Worked themselves smooth and smaller in a sparkle

Of shallow, hurrying barley-sugar water
Where minnows schooled that we scared when we played—
An eternity that ended once a tractor
Dropped its link-box in the gravel bed

And cement mixers began to come to life
And men in dungarees, like captive shades,
Mixed concrete, loaded, wheeled, turned, wheeled, as if
The Pharaoh's brickyards burned inside their heads.

*

Hoard and praise the verity of gravel.
Gems for the undeluded. Milt of earth.
Its plain, champing song against the shovel
Soundtests and sandblasts words like 'honest worth'.

Beautiful in or out of the river,
The kingdom of gravel was inside you too—
Deep down, far back, clear water running over
Pebbles of caramel, hailstone, mackerel-blue.

But the actual washed stuff kept you slow and steady
As you went stooping with your barrow full
Into an absolution of the body,
The shriven life tired bones and marrow feel.

So walk on air against your better judgement
Establishing yourself somewhere in between
Those solid batches mixed with grey cement
And a tune called 'The Gravel Walks' that conjures green.

Whitby-sur-Moyola

Caedmon too I was lucky to have known,
Back *in situ* there with his full bucket
And armfuls of clean straw, the perfect yardman,
Unabsorbed in what he had to do
But doing it perfectly, and watching you.
He had worked his angel stint. He was hard as nails
And all that time he'd been poeting with the harp
His real gift was the big ignorant roar
He could still let out of him, just bogging in
As if the sacred subjects were a herd
That had broken out and needed rounding up.
I never saw him once with his hands joined
Unless it was a case of eyes to heaven
And the quick sniff and test of fingertips
After he'd passed them through a sick beast's water.
Oh, Caedmon was the real thing all right.

'Poet's Chair'

for Carolyn Mulholland

Leonardo said: the sun has never
Seen a shadow. Now watch the sculptor move
Full circle round her next work, like a lover
In the sphere of shifting angles and fixed love.

I

Angling shadows of itself are what
Your 'Poet's Chair' stands to and rises out of
In its sun-stalked inner-city courtyard.
On the *qui vive* all the time, its four legs land
On their feet—cat's-foot, goat-foot, big soft splay-foot too;
Its straight back sprouts two bronze and leafy saplings.
Every flibbertigibbet in the town,
Old birds and boozers, late-night pissers, kissers,
All have a go at sitting on it some time.
It's the way the air behind them's winged and full,
The way a graft has seized their shoulderblades
That makes them happy. Once out of nature,
They're going to come back in leaf and bloom
And angel step. Or something like that. *Leaves*
On a bloody chair! Would you believe it?

II

Next thing I see the chair in a white prison
With Socrates sitting on it, bald as a coot,
Discoursing in bright sunlight with his friends.
His time is short. The day his trial began
A verdant boat sailed for Apollo's shrine
In Delos, for the annual rite
Of commemoration. Until its wreathed
And creepered rigging re-enters Athens
Harbour, the city's life is holy.

No executions. No hemlock bowl. No tears
And none now as the poison does its work
And the expert jailer talks the company through
The stages of the numbness. Socrates
At the centre of the city and the day
Has proved the soul immortal. The bronze leaves
Cannot believe their ears, it is so silent.
Soon Crito will have to close his eyes and mouth,
But for the moment everything's an ache
Deferred, foreknown, imagined and most real.

III

My father's ploughing one, two, three, four sides
Of the lea ground where I sit all-seeing
At centre field, my back to the thorn tree
They never cut. The horses are all hoof
And burnished flank, I am all foreknowledge.
Of the poem as a ploughshare that turns time
Up and over. Of the chair in leaf
The fairy thorn is entering for the future.
Of being here for good in every sense.

The Swing

Fingertips just tipping you would send you
Every bit as far—once you got going—
As a big push in the back.
                              Sooner or later,
We all learned one by one to go sky high,
Backward and forward in the open shed,
Toeing and rowing and jack-knifing through air.

*

Not Fragonard. Nor Brueghel. It was more
Hans Memling's light of heaven off green grass,
Light over fields and hedges, the shed-mouth
Sunstruck and expectant, the bedding-straw
Piled to one side, like a Nativity
Foreground and background waiting for the figures.
And then, in the middle ground, the swing itself
With an old lopsided sack in the loop of it,
Perfectly still, hanging like pulley-slack,
A lure let down to tempt the soul to rise.

*

Even so, we favoured the earthbound. She
Sat there as majestic as an empress
Steeping her swollen feet one at a time
In the enamel basin, feeding it
Every now and again with an opulent
Steaming arc from a kettle on the floor
Beside her. The plout of that was music
To our ears, her smile a mitigation.
Whatever light the goddess had once shone
Around her favourite coming from the bath
Was what was needed then: there should have been
Fresh linen, ministrations by attendants,
Procession and amazement. Instead, she took

Each rolled elastic stocking and drew it on
Like the life she would not fail and was not
Meant for. And once, when she'd scoured the basin,
She came and sat to please us on the swing,
Neither out of place nor in her element,
Just tempted by it for a moment only,
Half-retrieving something half-confounded.
Instinctively we knew to let her be.

*

To start up by yourself, you hitched the rope
Against your backside and backed on into it
Until it tautened, then tiptoed and drove off
As hard as possible. You hurled a gathered thing
From the small of your own back into the air.
Your head swept low, you heard the whole shed creak.

*

We all learned one by one to go sky high.
Then townlands vanished into aerodromes,
Hiroshima made light of human bones,
Concorde's neb migrated towards the future.
So who were we to want to hang back there
In spite of all?
                      In spite of all, we sailed
Beyond ourselves and over and above
The rafters aching in our shoulderblades,
The give and take of branches in our arms.

Two Stick Drawings

I

Claire O'Reilly used her granny's stick—
A crook-necked one—to snare the highest briars
That always grew the ripest blackberries.
When it came to gathering, Persephone
Was in the halfpenny place compared to Claire.
She'd trespass and climb gates and walk the railway
Where sootflakes blew into convolvulus
And the train tore past with the stoker yelling
Like a balked king from his iron chariot.

II

With its drover's cranes and blackthorns and ashplants,
The ledge of the back seat of my father's car
Had turned into a kind of stick-shop window,
But the only one who ever window-shopped
Was Jim of the hanging jaw, for Jim was simple
And rain or shine he'd make his desperate rounds
From windscreen to back window, hands held up
To both sides of his face, peering and groaning.
So every now and then the sticks would be
Brought out for him and stood up one by one
Against the front mudguard; and one by one
Jim would take the measure of them, sight
And wield and slice and poke and parry
The unhindering air; until he found
The true extension of himself in one
That made him jubilant. He'd run and crow,
Stooped forward, with his right elbow stuck out
And the stick held horizontal to the ground,
Angled across in front of him, as if
He were leashed to it and it drew him on
Like a harness rod of the inexorable.

A Call

'Hold on,' she said, 'I'll just run out and get him.
The weather here's so good, he took the chance
To do a bit of weeding.'
                              So I saw him
Down on his hands and knees beside the leek rig,
Touching, inspecting, separating one
Stalk from the other, gently pulling up
Everything not tapered, frail and leafless,
Pleased to feel each little weed-root break,
But rueful also . . .
                          Then found myself listening to
The amplified grave ticking of hall clocks
Where the phone lay unattended in a calm
Of mirror glass and sunstruck pendulums . . .

And found myself then thinking: if it were nowadays,
This is how Death would summon Everyman.

Next thing he spoke and I nearly said I loved him.

The Errand

'On you go now! Run, son, like the devil
And tell your mother to try
To find me a bubble for the spirit level
And a new knot for this tie.'

But still he was glad, I know, when I stood my ground,
Putting it up to him
With a smile that trumped his smile and his fool's errand,
Waiting for the next move in the game.

A Dog Was Crying Tonight in Wicklow Also

in memory of Donatus Nwoga

When human beings found out about death
They sent the dog to Chukwu with a message:
They wanted to be let back to the house of life.
They didn't want to end up lost forever
Like burnt wood disappearing into smoke
Or ashes that get blown away to nothing.
Instead, they saw their souls in a flock at twilight
Cawing and headed back for the same old roosts
And the same bright airs and wing-stretchings each morning.
Death would be like a night spent in the wood:
At first light they'd be back in the house of life.
(The dog was meant to tell all this to Chukwu.)

But death and human beings took second place
When he trotted off the path and started barking
At another dog in broad daylight just barking
Back at him from the far bank of a river.

And that is how the toad reached Chukwu first,
The toad who'd overheard in the beginning
What the dog was meant to tell. 'Human beings,' he said
(And here the toad was trusted absolutely),
'Human beings want death to last forever.'

Then Chukwu saw the people's souls in birds
Coming towards him like black spots off the sunset
To a place where there would be neither roosts nor trees
Nor any way back to the house of life.
And his mind reddened and darkened all at once
And nothing that the dog would tell him later
Could change that vision. Great chiefs and great loves
In obliterated light, the toad in mud,
The dog crying out all night behind the corpse house.

The Strand

The dotted line my father's ashplant made
On Sandymount Strand
Is something else the tide won't wash away.

The Walk

Glamoured the road, the day, and him and her
And everywhere they took me. When we stepped out
Cobbles were riverbed, the Sunday air
A high stream-roof that moved in silence over
Rhododendrons in full bloom, foxgloves
And hemlock, robin-run-the-hedge, the hedge
With its deckled ivy and thick shadows—
Until the riverbed itself appeared,
Gravelly, shallowy, summery with pools,
And made a world rim that was not for crossing.
Love brought me that far by the hand, without
The slightest doubt or irony, dry-eyed
And knowledgeable, contrary as be damned;
Then just kept standing there, not letting go.

*

So here is another longshot. Black and white.
A negative this time, in dazzle-dark,
Smudge and pallor where we make out you and me,
The selves we struggled with and struggled out of,
Two shades who have consumed each other's fire,
Two flames in sunlight that can sear and singe,
But seem like wisps of enervated air,
After-wavers, feathery ether-shifts . . .
Yet apt still to rekindle suddenly
If we find along the way charred grass and sticks
And an old fire-fragrance lingering on,
Erotic woodsmoke, witchery, intrigue,
Leaving us none the wiser, just better primed
To speed the plough again and feed the flame.

At the Wellhead

Your songs, when you sing them with your two eyes closed
As you always do, are like a local road
We've known every turn of in the past—
That midge-veiled, high-hedged side-road where you stood
Looking and listening until a car
Would come and go and leave you lonelier
Than you had been to begin with. So, sing on,
Dear shut-eyed one, dear far-voiced veteran,

Sing yourself to where the singing comes from,
Ardent and cut off like our blind neighbour
Who played the piano all day in her bedroom.
Her notes came out to us like hoisted water
Ravelling off a bucket at the wellhead
Where next thing we'd be listening, hushed and awkward.

*

That blind-from-birth, sweet-voiced, withdrawn musician
Was like a silver vein in heavy clay.
Night water glittering in the light of day.
But also just our neighbour, Rosie Keenan.
She touched our cheeks. She let us touch her braille
In books like books wallpaper patterns came in.
Her hands were active and her eyes were full
Of open darkness and a watery shine.

She knew us by our voices. She'd say she 'saw'
Whoever or whatever. Being with her
Was intimate and helpful, like a cure
You didn't notice happening. When I read
A poem with Keenan's well in it, she said,
'I can see the sky at the bottom of it now.'

At Banagher

Then all of a sudden there appears to me
The journeyman tailor who was my antecedent:
Up on a table, cross-legged, ripping out

A garment he must recut or resew,
His lips tight back, a thread between his teeth,
Keeping his counsel always, giving none,

His eyelids steady as wrinkled horn or iron.
Self-absenting, both migrant and ensconced;
Admitted into kitchens, into clothes

His touch has the power to turn to cloth again—
All of a sudden he appears to me,
Unopen, unmendacious, unillumined.

*

So more power to him on the job there, ill at ease
Under my scrutiny in spite of years
Of being inscrutable as he threaded needles

Or matched the facings, lining, hems and seams.
He holds the needle just off centre, squinting,
And licks the thread and licks and sweeps it through,

Then takes his time to draw both ends out even,
Plucking them sharply twice. Then back to stitching.
Does he ever question what it all amounts to

Or ever will? Or care where he lays his head?
My Lord Buddha of Banagher, the way
Is opener for your being in it.

Tollund

That Sunday morning we had travelled far.
We stood a long time out in Tollund Moss:
The low ground, the swart water, the thick grass
Hallucinatory and familiar.

A path through Jutland fields. Light traffic sound.
Willow bushes; rushes; bog-fir grags
In a swept and gated farmyard; dormant quags.
And silage under wraps in its silent mound.

It could have been a still out of the bright
'Townland of Peace', that poem of dream farms
Outside all contention. The scarecrow's arms
Stood open opposite the satellite

Dish in the paddock, where a standing stone
Had been resituated and landscaped,
With tourist signs in *futhark* runic script
In Danish and in English. Things had moved on.

It could have been Mulhollandstown or Scribe.
The by-roads had their names on them in black
And white; it was user-friendly outback
Where we stood footloose, at home beyond the tribe,

More scouts than strangers, ghosts who'd walked abroad
Unfazed by light, to make a new beginning
And make a go of it, alive and sinning,
Ourselves again, free-willed again, not bad.

September 1994

Postscript

And some time make the time to drive out west
Into County Clare, along the Flaggy Shore,
In September or October, when the wind
And the light are working off each other
So that the ocean on one side is wild
With foam and glitter, and inland among stones
The surface of a slate-grey lake is lit
By the earthed lightning of a flock of swans,
Their feathers roughed and ruffling, white on white,
Their fully grown headstrong-looking heads
Tucked or cresting or busy underwater.
Useless to think you'll park and capture it
More thoroughly. You are neither here nor there,
A hurry through which known and strange things pass
As big soft buffetings come at the car sideways
And catch the heart off guard and blow it open.

Crediting Poetry

The Nobel Lecture

[1 9 9 5]

When I first encountered the name of the city of Stockholm, I little thought that I would ever visit it, never mind end up being welcomed to it as a guest of the Swedish Academy and the Nobel Foundation. At that particular time, such an outcome was not just beyond expectation: it was simply beyond conception. In the nineteen-forties, when I was the eldest child of an ever-growing family in rural County Derry, we crowded together in the three rooms of a traditional thatched farmstead and lived a kind of den-life which was more or less emotionally and intellectually proofed against the outside world. It was an intimate, physical, creaturely existence in which the night sounds of the horse in the stable beyond one bedroom wall mingled with the sounds of adult conversation from the kitchen beyond the other. We took in everything that was going on, of course—rain in the trees, mice on the ceiling, a steam train rumbling along the railway line one field back from the house—but we took it in as if we were in the doze of hibernation. Ahistorical, pre-sexual, in suspension between the archaic and the modern, we were as susceptible and impressionable as the drinking water that stood in a bucket in our scullery: every time a passing train made the earth shake, the surface of that water used to ripple delicately, concentrically, and in utter silence.

But it was not only the earth that shook for us: the air around and above us was alive and signalling also. When a wind stirred in the beeches, it also stirred an aerial wire attached to the topmost branch of the chestnut tree. Down it swept, in through a hole bored in the corner of the kitchen window, right on into the innards of our wireless set where a little pandemonium of burbles and squeaks would suddenly give way to the voice of a BBC newsreader speaking out of the unexpected like a *deus ex machina*. And that voice too we could hear in our bedroom, transmitting from beyond and behind the voices of the adults in the kitchen; just as we could often hear, behind and beyond every voice, the frantic, piercing signalling of Morse code.

We could pick up the names of neighbours being spoken in the local accents of our parents, and in the resonant English tones of the newsreader the names of bombers and of cities bombed, of war fronts and army divisions, the numbers of planes lost and of prisoners taken, of casualties suffered and advances made; and always, of course, we would pick up too those other, solemn and oddly bracing words, 'the enemy' and 'the allies'. But even so, none of the news of these world-spasms entered me as terror. If there was something ominous in the newscaster's tones, there was something torpid about our understanding of what was at stake; and if there was something culpable about such political ignorance in that time and place, there was something positive about the security I inhabited as a result of it.

The wartime, in other words, was pre-reflective time for me. Pre-literate too. Pre-historical in its way. Then as the years went on and my listening became more deliberate, I would climb up on an arm of our big sofa to get my ear closer to the wireless speaker. But it was still not the news that interested me; what I was after was the thrill of story, such as a detective serial about a British special agent called Dick Barton or perhaps a radio adaptation of one of Capt. W. E. Johns's adventure tales about an RAF flying ace called Biggles. Now that the other children were older and there was so much going on in the kitchen, I had to get close to the actual radio set in order to concentrate my hearing, and in that intent proximity to the dial I grew familiar with the names of foreign stations, with Leipzig and Oslo and Stuttgart and Warsaw and, of course, with Stockholm.

I also got used to hearing short bursts of foreign languages as the dial hand swept round from the BBC to Radio Eireann, from the intonations of London to those of Dublin, and even though I did not understand what was being said in those first encounters with the gutturals and sibilants of European speech, I had already begun a journey into the wideness of the world. This in turn became a journey into the wideness of language, a journey where each point of arrival—whether in one's poetry or one's life—turned out to be a stepping stone rather than a destination, and it is that journey which has brought me now to this honoured spot. And yet the platform here feels more like a space station than a stepping stone, so that is why, for once in my life, I am permitting myself the luxury of walking on air.

I credit poetry for making this space-walk possible. I credit it immediately because of a line I wrote fairly recently encouraging myself (and whoever else might be listening) to 'walk on air against your better judgement'. But I credit it ultimately because poetry can make an order as true to the impact of external reality and as sensitive to the inner laws of the poet's being as the ripples that rippled in and rippled out across the water in that scullery bucket fifty years ago. An order where we can at last grow up to that which we stored up as we grew. An order which satisfies all that is appetitive in the intelligence and prehensile in the affections. I credit poetry, in other words, both for being itself and for being a help, for making possible a fluid and restorative relationship between the mind's centre and its circumference, between the child gazing at the word 'Stockholm' on the face of the radio dial and the man facing the faces that he meets in Stockholm at this most privileged moment. I credit it because credit is due to it, in our time and in all time, for its truth to life, in every sense of that phrase.

To begin with, I wanted that truth to life to possess a concrete reality, and rejoiced most when the poem seemed most direct, an upfront representation of the world it stood in for or stood up for or stood its ground against. Even as a schoolboy, I loved John Keats's ode 'To Autumn' for being an ark of the covenant between language and sensation; as an adolescent, I loved Gerard Manley Hopkins for the intensity of his exclamations, which were also equations for a rapture and an ache I didn't fully know I knew until I read him; I loved Robert Frost for his farmer's accuracy and his wily down-to-earthness; and Chaucer too for much the same reasons. Later on I would find a different kind of accuracy, a moral down-to-earthness to which I responded deeply and always will, in the war poetry of Wilfred Owen, a poetry where a New Testament sensibility suffers and absorbs the shock of the new century's barbarism. Then later again, in the pure consequence of Elizabeth Bishop's style, in the sheer obduracy of Robert Lowell's and in the barefaced confrontation of Patrick Kavanagh's, I encountered further reasons for believing in poetry's ability—and responsibility—to say what happens, to 'pity the planet', to be 'not concerned with Poetry'.

This temperamental disposition towards an art that was earnest and devoted to things as they are was corroborated by the experience of having been born and brought up in Northern Ireland and of having lived with that place even though I have lived out of it for the past quarter of a century. No place in the world prides itself more on its vigilance and realism, no place considers itself more qualified to censure any flourish of rhetoric or extravagance of aspiration. So, partly as a result of having internalized these attitudes through growing up with them, I went for years half-avoiding and half-resisting the opulence and extensiveness of poets as different as Wallace Stevens and Rainer Maria Rilke; crediting insufficiently the crystalline inwardness of Emily Dickinson, all those forked lightnings and fissures of association; and missing the visionary strangeness of Eliot. And these more or less costive attitudes were fortified by a refusal to grant the poet any more licence than any other citizen; and they were further induced by having to conduct oneself as a poet in a situation of ongoing political violence and public expectation. A public expectation, it has to be said, not of poetry as such but of political positions variously approvable by mutually disapproving groups.

In such circumstances, the mind still longs to repose in what Samuel Johnson once called with superb confidence 'the stability of truth', even as it recognizes the destabilizing nature of its own operations and enquiries. Without needing to be theoretically instructed, consciousness quickly realizes that it is the site of variously contending discourses. The child in the bedroom listening simultaneously to the domestic idiom of his Irish home and the official idioms of the British broadcaster while picking up from behind both the signals of some other distress, that child was already being schooled for the complexities of his adult predicament, a future where he would have to adjudicate among promptings variously ethical, aesthetical, moral, political, metrical, sceptical, cultural, topical, typical, post-colonial and, taken all together, simply impossible. So it was that I found myself in the mid-nineteen-seventies in another small house, this time in County Wicklow south of Dublin, with a young family of my own and a slightly less imposing radio set, listening to the rain in the trees and to the news of bombings closer to home—not only those by the Provisional IRA in Belfast but equally atrocious assaults in Dublin by loyalist paramilitaries from the north. Feeling puny in my predicaments as I read about the tragic logic of Osip Mandelstam's fate in the nineteen-thirties, feeling challenged yet steadfast in my non-combatant status when I heard, for example, that one particularly sweet-natured school friend had been interned without trial because he was suspected of having been involved in a political killing. What I was longing for was not quite stability but an active escape from the quicksand of relativism, a way of crediting poetry without anxiety or apology. In a poem called 'Exposure' I wrote then:

If I could come on meteorite!
Instead I walk through damp leaves,
Husks, the spent flukes of autumn,

Imagining a hero
On some muddy compound,
His gift like a slingstone
Whirled for the desperate.

How did I end up like this?
I often think of my friends'
Beautiful prismatic counselling
And the anvil brains of some who hate me

As I sit weighing and weighing
My responsible *tristia*.
For what? For the ear? For the people?
For what is said behind-backs?

Rain comes down through the alders,
Its low conducive voices
Mutter about let-downs and erosions
And yet each drop recalls

The diamond absolutes.
I am neither internee nor informer;
An inner émigré, grown long-haired
And thoughtful; a wood-kerne

Escaped from the massacre,
Taking protective colouring
From bole and bark, feeling
Every wind that blows;

Who, blowing up these sparks
For their meagre heat, have missed
The once-in-a-lifetime portent,
The comet's pulsing rose.

In one of the poems best known to students in my generation, a poem which could be said to have taken the nutrients of the symbolist movement and made them available in capsule form, the American poet Archibald MacLeish affirmed that 'A poem should be equal to / not true'. As a defiant statement of poetry's gift for telling truth but telling it slant, this is both cogent and corrective. Yet there are times when a deeper need enters, when we want the poem to be not only pleasurably right but compellingly wise, not only a surprising variation played upon the world, but a retuning of the world itself. We want the surprise to be transitive, like the impatient thump which unexpectedly restores the picture to the television set, or the electric shock which sets the fibrillating heart back to its proper rhythm. We want what the woman wanted in the prison queue in Leningrad, standing there blue with cold and whispering for fear, enduring the terror of Stalin's regime and asking the poet Anna Akhmatova if she could describe it all, if her art could be equal to it. And this is the want I too was experiencing in those far more protected circumstances in County Wicklow when I wrote the lines I have just quoted, a need for poetry that would merit the definition of it I gave a few moments ago, as an order 'true to the impact of external reality and . . . sensitive to the inner laws of the poet's being'.

The external reality and inner dynamic of happenings in Northern Ireland between 1968 and 1974 were symptomatic of change, violent change admittedly, but change nevertheless, and for the minority living there, change had been long overdue. It should have come early, as the result of the ferment of protest on the streets in the late sixties, but that was not to be and the eggs of danger which were always incubating got hatched out very quickly. While the Christian moralist in oneself was impelled to deplore the atrocious nature of the IRA's campaign of bombings and killings, and the 'mere Irish' in oneself was appalled by the ruthlessness of the British Army on occasions like Bloody Sunday in Derry in 1972, the minority citizen in oneself, the one who had grown up conscious that his group was distrusted and discriminated against in all kinds of official and unofficial ways, this citizen's perception was at one with the poetic truth of the situation in recognizing that if life in Northern Ireland were ever really to flourish, change had to take place. But that citizen's perception was also at one with the truth in recognizing that the very brutality of the means by which the IRA was pursuing change was destructive of the trust upon which new possibilities would have to be based.

Nevertheless, until the British government caved in to the strong-arm tactics of the Ulster loyalist workers after the Sunningdale Conference in 1974, a well-disposed mind could still hope to make sense of the circumstances, to balance what was promising with what was destructive and do what W. B. Yeats had tried to do half a century before, namely, 'to hold in a single thought reality and justice'. After 1974, however, for the twenty long years between then and the ceasefires of August 1994, such a hope proved impossible. The violence from below was productive of nothing but a retaliatory violence from above, the dream of justice became subsumed into the callousness of reality, and people settled in to a quarter century of life-waste and spirit-waste, of hardening attitudes and narrowing possibilities that were the natural result of political solidarity, traumatic suffering and sheer emotional self-protectiveness.

One of the most harrowing moments in the whole history of the harrowing of the heart in Northern Ireland came when a minibus full of workers being driven home one January evening in 1976 was held up by armed and masked men and the occupants of the van ordered at gunpoint to line up at the side of the road. Then one of the masked executioners said to them, 'Any Catholics among you, step out here.' As it happened, this particular group, with one exception, were all Protestants, so the presumption must have been that the masked men were Protestant paramilitaries about to carry out a tit-for-tat sectarian killing of the Catholic as the odd man out, the one who would have been presumed to be in sympathy with the IRA and all its actions. It was a terrible moment for him, caught between dread and witness, but he did make a motion to step forward. Then, the story goes, in that split second of decision, and in the relative cover of the winter evening darkness, he felt the hand of the Protestant worker next to him take his hand and squeeze it in a signal that said no, don't move, we'll not betray you, nobody need know what faith or party you belong to. All in vain, however, for the man stepped out of the line; but instead of finding a gun at his temple, he was pushed away as the gunmen opened fire on those remaining in the line, for these were not Protestant terrorists, but members, presumably, of the Provisional IRA.

It is difficult at times to repress the thought that history is about as instructive as an abattoir; that Tacitus was right and that peace is merely the desolation left behind after the decisive operations of merciless power. I remember, for example, shocking myself with a thought I had about that friend who was imprisoned in the seventies upon suspicion of having been involved with a political murder: I shocked myself by thinking that even if he were guilty, he might still perhaps be helping the future to be born, breaking the repressive forms and liberating new potential in the only way that worked, that is to say the violent way—which therefore became, by extension, the right way. It was like a moment of exposure to interstellar cold, a reminder of the scary element, both inner and outer, in which human beings envisage and conduct their lives. But it was only a moment. The birth of the future we desire is surely in the contraction which that terrified Catholic felt on the roadside when another hand gripped his hand, not in the gunfire that followed, so absolute and so desolate, if also so much a part of the music of what happens.

As writers and readers, as sinners and citizens, our realism and our aesthetic sense make us wary of crediting the positive note. The very gunfire braces us and the atrocious confers a worth upon the effort which it calls forth to confront it. We are rightly in awe of the torsions in the poetry of Paul Celan and rightly enamoured of the suspiring voice in Samuel Beckett because these are evidence that art can rise to the occasion and somehow be the corollary of Celan's stricken destiny as Holocaust survivor and Beckett's demure heroism as a member of the French Resistance. Likewise, we are rightly suspicious of that which gives too much consolation in these circumstances; the very extremity of our late-twentieth-century knowledge puts much of our cultural heritage to an extreme test. Only the very stupid or the very deprived can any longer help knowing that the documents of civilization have been written in blood and tears, blood and tears no less real for being very remote. And when this intellectual predisposition coexists with the actualities of Ulster and Israel and Bosnia and Rwanda and a host of other wounded spots on the face of the earth, the inclination is not only not to credit human nature with much constructive potential but not to credit anything too positive in the work of art.

Which is why for years I was bowed to the desk like some monk bowed over his prie-dieu, some dutiful contemplative pivoting his understanding in an attempt to bear his portion of the weight of the world, knowing himself incapable of heroic virtue or redemptive effect, but constrained by his obedience to his rule to repeat the effort and the posture. Blowing up sparks for a meagre heat. Forgetting faith, straining towards good works. Attending insufficiently to the diamond absolutes, among which must be counted the sufficiency of that which is absolutely imagined. Then finally and happily, and not in obedience to the dolorous circumstances of my native place but in spite of them, I straightened up. I began a few years ago to try to make space in my reckoning and imagining for the marvellous as well as for the murderous. And once again I shall try to represent the import of that changed orientation with a story out of Ireland.

This is a story about another monk holding himself up valiantly in the posture of endurance. It is said that once upon a time St

Kevin was kneeling with his arms stretched out in the form of a cross in Glendalough, a monastic site not too far from where we lived in County Wicklow, a place which to this day is one of the most wooded and watery retreats in the whole of the country. Anyhow, as Kevin knelt and prayed, a blackbird mistook his outstretched hand for some kind of roost and swooped down upon it, laid a clutch of eggs in it and proceeded to nest in it as if it were the branch of a tree. Then, overcome with pity and constrained by his faith to love the life in all creatures great and small, Kevin stayed immobile for hours and days and nights and weeks, holding out his hand until the eggs hatched and the fledglings grew wings, true to life if subversive of common sense, at the intersection of natural process and the glimpsed ideal, at one and the same time a signpost and a reminder. Manifesting that order of poetry which is true to all that is appetitive in the intelligence and prehensile in the affections. An order where we can at last grow up to that which we stored up as we grew.

St Kevin's story is, as I say, a story out of Ireland. But it strikes me that it could equally well come out of India or Africa or the Arctic or the Americas. By which I do not mean merely to consign it to a typology of folktales, or to dispute its value by questioning its culture-bound status within a multi-cultural context. On the contrary, its trustworthiness and its travel-worthiness have to do with its local setting. Indeed, the whole conception strikes me rather as being another example of the kind of work I saw a few weeks ago in the small museum in Sparta, on the morning before the news of this year's Nobel prize in literature was announced.

This was art which sprang from a cult very different from the faith espoused by St Kevin. Yet in it there was a representation of a roosted bird and an entranced beast and a self-enrapturing man, except that this time the man was Orpheus and the rapture came from music rather than prayer. The work itself was a small carved relief and I could not help making a sketch of it; but neither could I help copying out the information typed on the card which accompanied and identified the exhibit. The image moved me because of its antiquity and durability, but the description on the card moved me also because it gave a name and credence to that which I see myself as having been engaged upon for the past three decades: 'Votive panel,' the identification card said, 'possibly set up to Orpheus by local poet. Local work of the Hellenistic period.'

Once again, I hope I am not being sentimental or simply fetishizing—as we have learnt to say—the local. I wish instead to suggest that images and stories of the kind I am invoking here do function as bearers of value. The century has witnessed the defeat of Nazism by force of arms; but the erosion of the Soviet regimes was caused, among other things, by the sheer persistence, beneath the imposed ideological conformity, of cultural values and psychic resistances of the kind that these stories and images enshrine. Even if we have learned to be rightly and deeply fearful of elevating the cultural forms and conservatisms of any nation into normative and exclusivist systems, even if we have terrible proof that pride in the ethnic and religious heritage can quickly degrade into the fascistic, our vigilance on that score should not displace our love and trust in the good of the indigenous *per se*. On the contrary, a trust in the staying power and travel-worthiness of such good should encourage us to credit the possibility of a world where respect for the validity of every tradition will issue in the creation and maintenance of a salubrious political space. In spite of devastating and repeated acts of massacre, assassination and extirpation, the huge acts of faith which have marked the new relations between Palestinians and Israelis, Africans and Afrikaaners, and the way in which walls have come down in Europe and iron curtains have opened, all this inspires a hope that new possibility can still open up in Ireland as well. The crux of that problem involves an ongoing partition of the island between British and Irish jurisdictions, and an equally persistent partition of the affections in Northern Ireland between the British and Irish heritages; but surely every dweller in the country must hope that the governments involved in its governance can devise institutions which will allow that partition to become a bit more like the net on a tennis court, a demarcation allowing for agile give-and-take, for encounter and contending, prefiguring a future where the vitality that flowed in the beginning from those bracing words 'enemy' and 'allies' might finally derive from a less binary and altogether less binding vocabulary.

When the poet W. B. Yeats stood on this platform more than seventy years ago, Ireland was emerging from the throes of a traumatic civil war that had followed fast on the heels of a war of independence fought against the British. The struggle that ensued had been brief enough; it was over by May 1923, some seven months before Yeats sailed to Stockholm, but it was bloody, savage and intimate, and for generations to come it would dictate the terms of politics within the twenty-six independent counties of Ireland, that part of the island known first of all as the Irish Free State and then subsequently as the Republic of Ireland.

Yeats barely alluded to the civil war or the war of independence in his Nobel speech. Nobody understood better than he the connection between the construction or destruction of a political order and the founding or foundering of cultural life, but on this occasion he chose to talk instead about the Irish Dramatic Movement. His story was about the creative purpose of that movement and its historic good fortune in having not only his own genius to sponsor it, but also the genius of his friends John Millington Synge and Lady Augusta Gregory. He came to Sweden to tell the world that the local work of poets and dramatists had been as important to the transformation of his native place and times as the ambushes of guerrilla armies; and his boast in that elevated prose was essentially the same as the one he would make in verse more than a decade later in his poem 'The Municipal Gallery Revisited'. There Yeats presents himself among the portraits and heroic narrative paintings which celebrate the events and personalities of recent history and all of a sudden realizes that something truly epochmaking has occurred: ' "This is not," I say, / "The dead Ireland of my youth, but an Ireland / The poets have imagined, terrible and gay." ' And the poem concludes with two of the most quoted lines of his entire oeuvre:

Think where man's glory most begins and ends,
And say my glory was I had such friends.

And yet, expansive and thrilling as these lines are, they are an instance of poetry flourishing itself rather than proving itself, they are the poet's lap of honour, and in this respect if in no other they resemble what I am doing in this lecture. In fact, I should also quote here on my own behalf some other words from the poem: 'You that would judge me, do not judge alone / This book or that.' Instead, I ask you to do what Yeats asked his audience to do and think of the achievement of Irish poets and dramatists and novelists over the past forty years, among whom I am proud to count great friends. In literary matters, Ezra Pound advised against accepting the opinion of those 'who haven't themselves produced notable work', and it is advice I have been privileged to follow, since it is the good opinion of notable workers—and not just those in my own country—that has fortified my endeavour since I began to write in Belfast more than thirty years ago.

Yeats, however, was by no means all flourish. To the credit of poetry in our century there must surely be entered in any reckoning his two great sequences of poems entitled 'Nineteen Hundred and Nineteen' and 'Meditations in Time of Civil War', the latter of which contains the famous lyric about the bird's nest at his window, where a starling or stare had built in a crevice of the old wall. The poet was living then in a Norman tower which had been very much a part of the military history of the country in earlier times, and as his thoughts turned upon the irony of civilizations being consolidated by violent and powerful conquerors who end up commissioning the artists and the architects, he began to associate the sight of a mother bird feeding its young with the image of the honey-bee, an image deeply lodged in poetic tradition and always suggestive of the ideal of an industrious, harmonious, nurturing commonwealth:

> The bees build in the crevices
> Of loosening masonry, and there
> The mother birds bring grubs and flies.
> My wall is loosening; honey-bees,
> Come build in the empty house of the stare.
>
> We are closed in, and the key is turned
> On our uncertainty; somewhere

A man is killed, or a house burned,
Yet no clear fact to be discerned:
Come build in the empty house of the stare.

A barricade of stone or of wood;
Some fourteen days of civil war;
Last night they trundled down the road
That dead young soldier in his blood:
Come build in the empty house of the stare.

We had fed the heart on fantasies,
The heart's grown brutal from the fare;
More substance in our enmities
Than in our love; O honey-bees,
Come build in the empty house of the stare.

I have heard this poem repeated often, in whole and in part, by
people in Ireland over the past twenty-five years, and no wonder,
for it is as tender-minded towards life itself as St Kevin was and
as tough-minded about what happens in and to life as Homer.
It knows that the massacre will happen again on the roadside,
that the workers in the minibus are going to be lined up and
shot down just after quitting time; but it also credits as a reality
the squeeze of the hand, the actuality of sympathy and protec-
tiveness between living creatures. It satisfies the contradictory
needs which consciousness experiences at times of extreme crisis,
the need on the one hand for a truth-telling that will be hard
and retributive, and on the other hand the need not to harden
the mind to a point where it denies its own yearnings for sweet-
ness and trust. It is a proof that poetry can be equal to *and* true
at the same time, an example of that completely adequate poetry
which the Russian woman sought from Anna Akhmatova and
which William Wordsworth produced at a corresponding mo-
ment of historical crisis and personal dismay almost exactly two
hundred years ago.

When the bard Demodocus sings of the fall of Troy and of the
slaughter that accompanied it, Odysseus weeps and Homer says
that his tears were like the tears of a wife on a battlefield weep-
ing for the death of a fallen husband. His epic simile continues:

At the sight of the man panting and dying there,
she slips down to enfold him, crying out;
then feels the spears, prodding her back and shoulders,
and goes bound into slavery and grief.
Piteous weeping wears away her cheeks:
but no more piteous than Odysseus' tears,
cloaked as they were, now, from the company.

Even today, three thousand years later, as we channel-surf over
so much live coverage of contemporary savagery, highly in-
formed but nevertheless in danger of growing immune, familiar
to the point of overfamiliarity with old newsreels of the con-
centration camp and the gulag, Homer's image can still bring
us to our senses. The callousness of those spear-shafts on the
woman's back and shoulders survives time and translation. The
image has that documentary adequacy which answers all that
we know about the intolerable.

But there is another kind of adequacy which is specific to
lyric poetry. This has to do with the 'temple inside our hear-
ing' which the passage of the poem calls into being. It is an
adequacy deriving from what Mandelstam called 'the steadfast-
ness of speech articulation', from the resolution and indepen-
dence which the entirely realized poem sponsors. It has as much
to do with the energy released by linguistic fission and fusion,
with the buoyancy generated by cadence and tone and rhyme
and stanza, as it has to do with the poem's concerns or the poet's
truthfulness. In fact, in lyric poetry, truthfulness becomes rec-
ognizable as a ring of truth within the medium itself. And it is
the unappeasable pursuit of this note, a note tuned to its most
extreme in Emily Dickinson and Paul Celan and orchestrated to
its most opulent in John Keats, it is this which keeps the poet's
ear straining to hear the totally persuasive voice behind all the
other informing voices.

Which is a way of saying that I have never quite climbed
down from the arm of that sofa. I may have grown more atten-
tive to the news and more alive to the world history and world-
sorrow behind it. But the thing uttered by the speaker I strain
towards is still not quite the story of what is going on; it is more
reflexive than that, because as a poet I am in fact straining
towards a strain, in the sense that the effort is to repose in the

stability conferred by a musically satisfying order of sounds. As if the ripple at its widest desired to be verified by a reformation of itself, to be drawn in and drawn out through its point of origin.

I also strain towards this in the poetry I read. And I find it, for example, in the repetition of that refrain of Yeats's, 'Come build in the empty house of the stare', with its tone of supplication, its pivots of strength in the words 'build' and 'house' and its acknowledgement of dissolution in the word 'empty'. I find it also in the triangle of forces held in equilibrium by the triple rhyme of 'fantasies' and 'enmities' and 'honey-bees', and in the sheer in-placeness of the whole poem as a given form within the language. Poetic form is both the ship and the anchor. It is at once a buoyancy and a holding, allowing for the simultaneous gratification of whatever is centrifugal and centripetal in mind and body. And it is by such means that Yeats's work does what the necessary poetry always does, which is to touch the base of our sympathetic nature while taking in at the same time the unsympathetic reality of the world to which that nature is constantly exposed. The form of the poem, in other words, is crucial to poetry's power to do the thing which always is and always will be to poetry's credit: the power to persuade that vulnerable part of our consciousness of its rightness in spite of the evidence of wrongness all around it, the power to remind us that we are hunters and gatherers of values, that our very solitudes and distresses are creditable, in so far as they, too, are an earnest of our veritable human being.

Index of Titles

Index of First Lines

Index of Titles

Index of First Lines